## ADVANCE PRAISE

"Stephen Kagawa is a person of high integrity and character who always puts others ahead of himself where service to others is the brand, not a by-product. *Aloha Financial Advising* is a must-read because it reflects Stephen's passionate desire to listen and analyze the client's needs and hopes. He then puts together a practical application of the latest in technology and market knowledge in pursuit of one's financial success."

—THE HONORABLE NORMAN MINETA, FORMER US SECRETARY OF TRANSPORTATION UNDER PRESIDENT GEORGE W. BUSH AND FORMER SECRETARY OF COMMERCE UNDER PRESIDENT BILL CLINTON

"Stephen has always focused on the care for others while providing leading financial advice. *Aloha Financial Advising* provides valuable insights on how to maximize the care for your clients as you serve them."

—DAVE WILKEN, PRESIDENT, LIFE, GLOBAL ATLANTIC FINANCIAL GROUP

*"Stephen is one of the leading agency builders in the United States. He is a third-generation agency leader who is recognized as an expert in the Asian-American marketplace."*

—JOSÉ S. SUQUET, CHAIRMAN OF THE BOARD, PRESIDENT & CEO, PAN-AMERICAN LIFE INSURANCE GROUP

*"Stephen is creative, innovative, and dynamic. In this book he shares insights that have propelled him to success."*

—ADELIA CHUNG, SPECTRUM WEALTH MANAGEMENT OWNER, MILLION DOLLAR ROUND TABLE PRESIDENT 2005

*"Stephen continues the legacy of his family through Aloha Financial Advising as an advocate for 'hands-on' financial planning to meet the individual needs of clients."*

—GEORGE HENNING, CHAIRMAN & PRESIDENT, PACIFIC GLOBAL INVESTMENT MANAGEMENT

*"Stephen distills a lifelong commitment to doing good and a values-based approach to leadership and decision making into the tools that you need to make smart decisions."*

—ANN BURROUGHS, PRESIDENT AND CEO, JAPANESE AMERICAN NATIONAL MUSEUM

*"Aloha Financial Advising is an innovative way for people to ensure financial security and peace of mind for those that mean the most to them. I trust and value Stephen's aloha spirit and his consultative approach to caring for his clients' financial needs wherever in the world their lives may lead."*

—ROY YAMAGUCHI, RESTAURATEUR AND FOUNDER OF ROY'S RESTAURANTS

# ALOHA FINANCIAL ADVISING

# ALOHA
## FINANCIAL ADVISING

### DOING GOOD TO DO BETTER FOR YOUR
### CLIENTS AND YOURSELF

Stephen Kagawa

**LIONCREST**
PUBLISHING

ALOHA FINANCIAL ADVISING
*Doing Good to Do Better for Your Clients and Yourself*

ISBN   978-1-5445-0446-9  *Hardcover*
       978-1-5445-0445-2  *Paperback*
       978-1-5445-0444-5  *Ebook*

*This book is for financial advisors who want to do better for their clients and want to do better for themselves. It's also for anyone who's feeling lost, or offtrack, or whose career doesn't reflect their true values. May the lessons in this book serve as a rudder to steer you toward the greatness that is already inside of you.*

# CONTENTS

# INTRODUCTION

This book is about the dynamic between financial advisors and their clients. More specifically, it's about how people interact differently with one another when the relationship is based on trust.

Relationships between financial advisors and their clients aren't always built on a foundation of trust, to the detriment of everyone involved. You don't have to subscribe to this dynamic. There is another way.

In this book, I'll tell you about the other way. From my perspective, it's not only what's right, it *works*. Clients and advisors get more of what they want, and they enjoy the process.

I believe in personally and intentionally shaping our values and relying on our character to inform the way we approach everything in life, including our business and consultative process. If in your work, you are purposefully driving your business forward with character as your rudder, then we're already in agreement.

My way isn't the only way to work with those who seek advice. You might be doing something completely different that works, and if that's the case, I'm not proposing you change it. My intention with this book is to help shape what you do and how you do it to reflect your best intentions even better. It's simple and effective, and I believe in it. It's one way of working with people for a better outcome.

Earning a person's trust—and honoring that trust—changes how you communicate with one another. This new dynamic, together with your core values and your education and expertise, takes you to the next level of financial advising. More than a salesperson, and even more than a trusted advisor, that trust empowers you to rise up and really *do good* to do better for your clients and yourself.

The key is seeing everyone as a human being with wants and desires that are often beyond what you have to offer in the way of products and services. You may not understand them initially or agree with them—ever. The only way to discover those wants is through conversations. This is how you uncover what's truly important to people so you can help them envision the best outcome they can imagine. Their best outcome can only *be* the best if it's based on their true wants—not what they *think* they want or have been led to believe they *should* want. The outcome you help them achieve must be based on what they *truly desire for their lives.*

Getting to this point with a prospect starts with your core values—what you believe about people—because that inevitably guides your behavior. It drives the dynamic you create with the people with whom you interact.

I want to talk to you about my core values. First, let's talk about the problems we face as financial advisors operating in a system that hasn't always valued trust.

## A SYSTEM THAT REWARDS BAD BEHAVIOR

I've been in this business for a long time and face the same problems you deal with. I know that financial advisors are stuck in a system that doesn't always benefit them or their clients financially, ethically, or in progressing either party toward a more fulfilling life. Does this sound familiar? It's all too common.

I hear this all the time from aspiring financial advisors on the insurance *and* the investment side: "I really want to help people."

Somehow, *helping* people quickly turns to *selling* people—more specifically, selling them products and services that may or may not satisfy their true desires. How they do this generally entails product selling, the direct use of sales concepts, the often called-upon "needs analysis," leading questions veiled behind consultative processes, and alarming headlines that shake people into action. After all, the definition of selling is "to persuade."

Don't get me wrong. There is a time and place to do these things. Completing a fact finder, sharing a dramatic story, and employing other sales techniques help move clients closer to getting what they want. Used properly, these concepts can serve clients, but when you use them simply to sell without focusing on the person you hope to serve, you are doing the person a disservice.

Nobody sets out to do this. No one gets into financial advising because they like to manipulate people. There are better ways to make a living.

The problem is, these methods—even when used improperly—not only work, they're rewarded. Selling insurance, investments, and other wealth management products, packages, and services through any means (including fear tactics) leads to fees, commissions, bonuses, and accolades. Advisors who successfully push enough product are put on a pedestal and admired by their peers, regardless of whether they've sacrificed their clients' happiness for the sake of the sale.

Not all transactions of this nature lead to undesirable outcomes. Surely, an individual who invests in a certain stock, mutual fund, or insurance policy may be better off than they would have been had they not made the purchase. Focusing on the product, though, ahead of what the person truly wants isn't what anyone who enters the financial industry sets out to accomplish. Advisors are just like everyone else, and they inherently want to do good and be good people. They want to treat others well. Somehow, the system shifts us in a different direction.

People shouldn't need to worry that their advisor is going to get them to buy something that won't get them to where they want to be in life. For goodness' sake, they're advisors, and "to advise" is supposed to be about offering recommendations as to one's best course of action. When it comes to planning for their future, don't they already have enough to worry about? For starters, we're all going to die. You, me, our prospects, and our clients. It's going to happen. How scary is that? Some of us will grow very old, and some will get very sick. Some of us will have to take care of loved ones who get very old and very sick. These are the realities of everyday life—the serious matters we *should* worry about. As financial advisors, we can talk about and prepare our clients for these realities. We can help them plan for these situations in an honest and open way so instead of creating stress, we're relieving it.

The travesty for advisors caught in a system that values sales over trust is that we might miss the opportunity to help people deal with the real issues in their lives. We can leave our clients ill-prepared and even jeopardize their happiness. Having conversations about what our clients will likely be dealing with and their hopeful outcomes when life happens to them opens the door to preparing them for the scary stuff in a productive way.

I don't know if this system will ever change. I do know that helping people take advantage of all the opportunities open to them while dealing with whatever challenges life brings them is one way to be an effective financial advisor. My experience has proven to me that we can be *even more successful* doing it this way. The onus is on us, as financial advisors, to take on that responsibility and enjoy successful careers while striving to do better for our clients.

We can do better for ourselves and for our clients. We can do better by doing good. That sounds so easy, right? It's not. It's harder than you think. I know because I've done it, and I believe you can do it, too. Once you learn how, you'll want to work with everyone in this way.

# BUILDING A SYSTEM THAT REWARDS DOING GOOD

Many companies have what they call *guiding principles* or *core values*. My colleagues and I live by both. Our guiding principles—client-centric, legal transparency, corporate and community citizenship, and non-competitive posturing—are strategic precepts that give us structure and direction for how we contract with vendors and other partners to position ourselves to best serve our clients. These principles do not waiver, regardless of the changing financial environment. They're how we do business.

This book is about something deeper than guiding principles. It's about the core values that guide our behavior—how we feel about our clients, and how we interact with them. This goes beyond the rules of business. It's about the assumptions we make about the people we know and those we have yet to meet. Values-based beliefs are the foundation of values-based relationships and are ultimately the key to becoming a values-based advisor. A true values-based advisor calls upon their wares to create and deliver a values-based experience in their advice and in every aspect of their practice. My decision to integrate my deep-rooted personal beliefs and aspirations into our business was a great leap of faith. Fortunately, my colleagues now embrace this philosophy and consider these core values to be our company's most valuable assets.

## YOUR GREATEST ASSETS

Our core values are based on five Hawaiian words: *Mahalo, Aloha, Ohana, Pono,* and *Imua.* While I'm not of Hawaiian blood and don't speak the Hawaiian language, I am part of a fourth generation of Kagawas born in the state of Hawaii. I can't help but selfishly make claims to its land and culture, and I've adopted these words and taken certain liberties in how we interpret them to represent our core values. With all due respect to true native Hawaiians and the sanctity of the meaning behind their beautiful language, these words closely align with the values I learned from my mother and my father. They also align perfectly with what I believe about how people can interact best with one another.

**Mahalo** means *thank you.* This is the word I use for living with gratitude and the importance of appreciating everything in my life. With Mahalo, you are grateful for the people in your life, and you appreciate their differences, too. You appreciate how they look at life and act in life, where they come from, and where they're going. You're thankful for the good fortune to meet many different people on life's journey. As a financial advisor, you deal with people from all walks of life with differing beliefs, opinions, and priorities and an endless array of opportunities to express Mahalo.

**Aloha** means many things, most commonly *hello* and *good-bye*. The meaning of Aloha I prefer defines how I seek to live and work. It's to do so *with love*. Deferring to the core value of Aloha insists on treating yourself and the people around you with love. You care for others and listen and share with them openly, willingly, and with hope. You understand that people and their opinions are neither right nor wrong and that they're simply different. Treating people with love or Aloha changes how you feel about them and makes you want to do your best for them.

**Ohana** means *family*. This core value guides me to treat other people the way I treat the members of my family. With Ohana, you are honest and forthright and never knowingly lead others astray. Sometimes Ohana means telling people things they don't want to hear yet *need* to hear for their own good, and you do it with the intent of helping them satisfy their desires—even when they can't see this for themselves. Sometimes, Ohana requires you to hold people accountable. It's not easy to do this, and people may not always agree with what you have to say. Again, think of how you treat your family. Think about how you speak with the people you care about the most. Your conversations aren't always agreeable, yet you dig in and have those talks anyway because you care about their outcomes. When you're truly committed to your clients, you treat them like Ohana. You're there for them not *only* when you're working together on their financial plan but whenever they need you. Your door is always open, you're always kind and welcoming, and you're also committed to being truthful. You may even treat your competitors like Ohana, with the same honesty and the same high expectations and accountability that you show family members.

**Pono** means *to do the right thing.* It means to live with righteousness—to do the right things for the right reasons. No one is perfect. If you seek to live your life with Pono, your good intentions in your plans and actions are certain to reflect your desire to do right.

**Imua** means *always move forward*—to keep learning and continuing to grow. With Imua, you evolve and become more skilled, more compassionate, and more valuable to yourself and to your clients and others with whom you interact. Moving forward may require you to change the way you do things, to confront people and problems, and to motivate yourself as well as others to take action. Anyone can be complacent. Imua takes heart, perseverance, and a certain amount of courage.

These core values are what I look to when I'm confronted with tough decisions. Having these in place and adhering to them makes my decisions easier. More importantly, it makes them right for me and for people who seek my counsel.

Your core values may be different. Whatever they are, think of them as your prized possessions and look to them as the moral code that guides your interactions with people, allowing these values to proactively and positively shape the way you approach others.

Some financial advisors worry that living by a code of conduct such as this will affect their ability to sell and make money. This is absolutely true, though perhaps not the way you might think. Adhering to core values actually *improves* your ability to make money. Over time, as you incorporate your values into how you serve people, *selling* becomes much easier. By selling, I don't mean convincing people they need to buy from you but rather building a relationship where people *want* to buy from you. Your prospects and clients sense honesty and good intentions, and they'll trust you. They will begin to actively seek you out for advice.

It's ideal that people feel they can come to you, confident that the advice you offer is based on *their* best interests, not yours. And whether you're in banking, insurance, investments, taxes, or law, they'll see you as their financial guiding light. You will become their lead financial advisor—not only a trusted advisor but a values-based, *Aloha Advisor*.

When you treat a person this way, going broad and deep to understand and appreciate what they want, doing so without judgment, and then identifying what they need to satisfy those wants, they'll come away with a very positive experience. They'll gladly write favorable reviews about you and provide you with testimonials. They'll eagerly share their experience with others, talking about you to their family, friends, and colleagues. They'll refer the people they respect and care about most to you.

In this book, I'll show you how my core values have played out throughout my career. Over and over, they continue to guide me toward becoming the financial advisor I aspire to be. That person clings to his values while inspiring others to do the same so that we can all serve each other in a way that allows us to live our most fulfilled lives. As you read this book, think about your own core values. What are they? What would you like them to be? How might your values affect your relationships with those you serve?

## SUSPECTS, PROSPECTS, CUSTOMERS, CLIENTS, AND ADVOCATES

I have many stories to share with you about my experiences as a financial advisor working with people who wanted something and who came to me or to another advisor to help them get it. While values are first and foremost in how I work with people, for the purpose of clarity, I believe it's important that you understand the different stages a person may be in within an advisor's professional relationship. In this book, I refer to people generally as "clients," and sometimes more specifically as "suspects," "prospects," "customers," "clients," and "advocates."

- A *suspect* is anyone in the world. They may or may not want or need the help of an advisor.
- A *prospect* is a person who is seeking help or clearly needs help whether or not they realize it. The extent to which they actually *want* help makes them a better prospect for the advisor.
- A *customer* is someone who wants a particular product or service and has already made up their mind that whatever it is they want to buy from an advisor is exactly what they need. The product may or may not fulfill a want. Once the individual makes the purchase, they are a customer.
- A *client*, on the other hand, sees the advisor as more of a consultant. The client is willing to share information with the advisor, consider their advice, and act on it by signing the papers and making the purchase or following whatever counsel is given.
- Finally, an *advocate* is a client who believes in their advisor so much that they refer people they care about and respect to the advisor. They're an ambassador for you, bringing people they want the best for to you and knowing they can count on you to deliver. *We need those who we serve to be our advocates.*

In the spirit of Aloha, sharing with others openly, willingly, and with hope, I want to help you do good for your suspects, prospects, customers, clients, and advocates and find your own professional and personal success and fulfillment. I'm not looking for you to be just like me—I want to inspire you to leverage who you are and what you know to surpass me. I know that you can and hope that you will.

Am I setting my sights too high? I don't think so. I learned early on that one person is capable of inspiring great change. *You* are capable of great change.

Let me tell you about a person who inspired me and many others in his own lifetime—my grandfather L. T. Kagawa. He showed me that we are all capable of much more than we might imagine.

### DOING GOOD TO DO BETTER FOR MANY: L. T. KAGAWA

In the 1930s, my grandfather Lawrence Takeo "L. T." Kagawa, a second-generation American, was working for a trust company in the Territory of Hawaii.

L. T. believed that everyone had the right to protect their assets. In his work, he noticed that people of color in Hawaii didn't necessarily have access to the same products that people across the rest of America readily utilized to do so. This was true not only for those of color in Hawaii; this was the fact for people of color *throughout the United States*. It was absolute when it came to obtaining life insurance coverage for their families. The policies available to his community were fewer than those available to his Caucasian neighbors and came with higher premiums than what they were paying.

He didn't think that was right, and he was motivated to do something about it. Keep in mind, this was more than twenty-five years before Hawaii gained statehood. More than 50 percent of the population of the territory was Asian, so most Hawaii residents didn't have access to the same types of coverage for the same price as what was being offered to Caucasian Americans.

Believing in the importance of this issue and understanding its sensitivities, L. T. decided to seek out a partner and instead found a champion and hero to further his cause. He traveled to San Francisco by boat, on the SS *Lurline*, in hopes of meeting a legendary Italian American man who was helping Italian immigrants in the United States. This man was offering these people loans so they could start businesses.

Even though my grandfather didn't have an appointment with this man, he went to his office, day after day, and sat in the lobby waiting for an opportunity to meet with him. At the end of each day, the secretary would escort him out.

On his final day on the mainland, L. T. appealed to the man's secretary:

"I know your boss is a very, very busy man," he said. "I traveled all the way from Hawaii to tell him about an opportunity based upon his philosophies. I really want just a few minutes to share my thoughts with him."

At the end of that day, the secretary said, "Mr. Kagawa, Mr. Giannini will see you."

After traveling more than 2,000 miles and days of sitting

patiently in the lobby of that San Francisco office, my grand-father was finally introduced to Amadeo Giannini.

"Mr. Kagawa, how go things in Tokyo?" he asked my grandfather.

L. T. responded, "Just fine, thank you. And how go things in Rome?"

They both laughed because, as sons of immigrants, they were not from Tokyo, Japan, or Rome, Italy. They were citizens of the United States. They were Americans.

My grandfather and inspiration, Lawrence Takeo "L. T." Kagawa. A photograph of Bank of America founder Amadeo "A.P." Giannini hangs on his office wall. My grandfather, with support from Mr. Giannini, initiated the abolishment of discriminatory underwriting practices in the life insurance industry in the 1930s.

The two hit it off immediately. Mr. Giannini recognized a chance for developing a business opportunity with my grandfather, and he challenged L. T. to gather relevant data to back up his findings.

My grandfather returned home, where he met with the head of the Department of Health in the Territory of Hawaii, Dr. Fred Trotter. Out of that meeting came studies of the mortality rates between the different ethnicities of people who lived in Hawaii. They found only a slight difference—the Asian population was actually *outliving* the Caucasian population.

L. T. shared that information with Mr. Giannini, who owned a small life insurance company amongst his vast holdings. Through that relationship, my grandfather initiated the abolishment of racially discriminatory underwriting practices in the United States by becoming the first person to provide equal opportunities for people of color in Hawaii in the form of life insurance coverage. That was way back in 1933.

Today, Mr. Giannini's life insurance company, the former Occidental Life of California, is known as Transamerica. Amadeo "A.P." Giannini, incidentally, also founded the Bank of Italy, which became Bank of America.

My grandfather wasn't yet an established leader. He was simply a diligent, hardworking man who saw a wrong and did what needed to be done to make it right.

In the 1930s, racial equality was a rarity. As late as the 1980s and early '90s, some of the biggest companies in the United States continued to support originally issued, racially discriminatory underwriting rates on their older policies on people of color. It's a sad reality of where we come from as a country. Yet one person found another, and another, and by building these relationships through hard work and perseverance, that man made a difference for many people he knew, and many more he'd never meet.

## RELATIONSHIPS THAT EXPAND YOUR INFLUENCE

I'm humbled by the accomplishments of my grandfather. His commitment to doing what's right and reaching out to others to help him in that effort show what's possible when people with similar values join forces to achieve greater goals for the greater good. L. T. inspired me to break away from the traditional financial services system and find my own path.

Breaking away from the system you're in *is* possible on your own. My preference is to collaborate with others, like my grandfather did. His life's work inspired me to start The Pacific Bridge Companies (TPBC), where I partner with other financial advisors whose guiding principles and core values align with my own: values like Mahalo, Aloha, Ohana, Pono, and Imua.

Whom you partner with is up to you, and chapter 8, "Working within a Collaborative to Deliver for Your Client," provides a full discussion of the benefits of formal and informal collaboratives. The key is to ensure you share the same principles for serving others. This way, you can leverage those relationships to expand your influence to do good, and do better, for yourself and your clients.

My platform for doing this is The Pacific Bridge Companies and its vision of helping financial advisors help their clients wherever in the world their lives may lead. People want global financial navigation, and through my company, TPBC, I'm doing my best to bring down the walls that separate countries in the financial world. Despite the differences between us—from culture to faith to politics and even the foods we eat and the languages we speak—at the heart and soul of things, we're much the same. We love our families. We want the best for them, and we want the best for our businesses and communities, too. The things that are most important to people are universal across the country and around the globe.

The Pacific Bridge Companies does this in two ways: first, through our system that continues to evolve between the United States and other countries, primarily centered on Asian countries, that closes gaps in the financial world. Second, we work with immigrants in the US. People come to America from about 200 countries, yet the current financial planning system in the United States is homogenous. Amazingly, US financial planning generally fails to consider where people come from or where they might be going. TPBC is shaping a new system for financial planning for this reality, aimed primarily at first-generation and ethnically Asian American communities. This system considers their country of origin and their potential destinations in life, and through it, wealth management strategies of worth can be delivered holistically.

I'm only one person with one company, and so we achieve this through a collaborative that provides us with a wealth of resources to identify and connect with specialists across banking, insurance, investment, tax, and law from different geographical regions for purposeful engagement to help those who are navigating around the globe. We partner with select collaborative members who meet our high standards of expertise within their industry so that no *one* collaborating company need recreate it. We celebrate the unique talents and abilities of those within the collaborative and represent a coordinated collective of cooperating competencies, assisting our clients toward the lives they seek together.

## MY ASPIRATIONAL VISION

My grandfather L. T. Kagawa gave his best to the world, and I hope to do the same by sharing my philosophy and my lessons with other financial advisors. Each day, I strive to live up to his vision of access and opportunity.

I have my own vision, too, an aspirational vision of the world as I imagine it, one that I believe I have the power to help shape with my ability and resolve. My "why," my purpose in life, is to help people who need my help, and to create that world. Inspired by people like Kathy, a single mother who taught me the importance of what I can do as a financial advisor, I envision a world where people are protected from the potentially devastating financial realities of inevitable human hardship, and sometimes tragedy.

I'll tell you Kathy's story in the next chapter. It gets to the heart of why Aloha Advisors do what we do—why I do what I do. This is about truly caring about other people enough to do more than you're used to, more than you have to, and sometimes more than you want to. It's about being true to your values.

My vision of global financial navigation and my missions of filling gaps and helping ethnic communities both pre- and post-immigration come from my heart and soul. They are bigger than life initiatives, and I realize they are greater than any one person could ever accomplish. But I continue to strive to make a difference for other people, the people who need me. I may never know the extent to which I can make a difference in someone else's life, but simply knowing that I am living each day by my core values, and the potential I have, as an Aloha Advisor, to help shape the world of my aspirational vision, drives me to not only accept but gladly welcome the challenges that each new day brings.

## ALOHA

This book isn't about what investments you should sell, what insurance company or products you should represent, or what trust, legal structure, or tax code you need to help your prospects and clients take advantage of. This is about helping people. It's about integrating what you personally believe in and value at your core into your business as you help them. It's about access, opportunity, and giving your best to the world. It's about doing your job in a way that allows people to enjoy more fulfilled lives because of you, their financial advisor.

Even though you may not subscribe to my way of thinking, I implore you to read what I have to say and think about how it could work for you. Whether or not you decide to adopt my mindset, methods, and style of financial advising, I hope this book inspires you to become more self-aware in how you interact with those who look to you for guidance. At the very least, take it upon yourself to look inside, see who you are, and decide who you want to be. Then align your wealth management practices accordingly.

Aloha means goodbye, and it also means hello. This is the beginning of our conversation, where I greet you and offer what I know about financial advisors, our clients, and the dynamic that exists between us. Doing good has allowed me to do better for other people and for myself. It's allowed me to grow closer to what I believe an Aloha Advisor should be. If this is your wish, too, I believe you'll find value in what I wish to share with you.

# 2

# HOW TRADITIONAL WEALTH MANAGEMENT MISSES THE MARK FOR ADVISORS

In Japan, it's customary for financial advisors to begin a conversation with their prospect by telling them all about their company. When I was first introduced to the business in the United States, I was taught to do the same.

Throughout the sales society, in wealth management and other industries around the globe, there's a tendency for the people selling to believe it's important to hang their hats on the accomplishments of the company they represent. They seek instant credibility and proudly carry the title of "VP," "financial consultant," or "financial advisor" for a big company that's been around awhile. This apparently proves them worthy to those they hope to motivate into becoming clients.

I could never understand why a person should trust me based on the history of the company that hired me. I don't think anyone should be immediately impressed by me or my company. I see the people I'm advising as my equals, and it is my responsibility to help them. To do the best job possible for them, I must ask questions. My prospects and clients don't always like the questions, yet I must ask them so they can articulate their reality, and together, we can appropriately confront it.

If I don't ask enough questions to learn, no matter how uncomfortable the conversation becomes, I might be tempted to fill in the blanks myself. The only information I'd have to fill in those blanks is what I already know—my assumptions.

Putting my company's name and my title aside to focus on the individual was hard at first. It would've been easier to go back to what I thought sales was supposed to be. I wasn't really that person, though, and I wouldn't feel right doing the job that way. I wouldn't be fulfilling my responsibility to these people who were trusting me to give them the best products and services behind properly arranged structures or give them sage advice that ensured a good outcome for them and their families. To do this, I had to trust my prospects and clients, and they had to learn to trust me.

I didn't start out creating this kind of dynamic with those who were open to meeting with me. I started the same way most financial advisors do. Sincerely understanding people and delivering the value of what I had to offer them came later in my career.

## LESSONS LEARNED AND SHARED: HANNAH AND KATHY

Moving from traditional financial advising to becoming an Aloha Advisor took time, and I was influenced by several people I met along the way.

Hannah was a teacher who was trying to sell life insurance on the side. She was aligned with a real estate seminar provider that taught people how to buy properties with no money down and sell them for a profit. There was an opportunity for her to offer financial planning expertise as part of the real estate seminar package to those who engaged in their system. She decided to initially become a full-time life insurance consultant with the company to do so.

At first, Hannah didn't feel right about what she was doing and how she was doing it, but she didn't know why. She was even thinking about giving up on the idea of being an insurance consultant or financial planner. Hannah knew I was helping people transform their financial planning practices, and she came to me for advice.

Earlier in my life, I didn't think much of life insurance salespeople. I had a stereotypical image of them as sleazy guys in loud suits who talked fast and ripped people off. When I first got into the insurance part of the business, I was secretly ashamed of what I was going to do for a living. It wasn't what I expected to do with my life, and back then I'd never have imagined someone like Hannah—an incredibly well-educated, smart, pleasant schoolteacher—*wanting* to actually sell insurance.

Fortunately, before Hannah came to me, I had learned that I had nothing to be ashamed of. My opinion of life insurance and the people who sell policies was changed by another woman named Kathy. She taught me a lesson that made me think very differently about what I do, and it's a lesson I've passed on to many others, including Hannah.

Kathy was one of my trainers during my initial internship at an insurance company. She graciously invited me over for dinner one evening. When I arrived, I was greeted by her two children. We played until dinner and, after tucking the kids into bed, Kathy told me that she had a story to tell me.

"Several years ago," she said, "my husband and I owned a small business in the garment district in Los Angeles. My husband was also a boxer, and he was a proud and handsome man. Well, one day some thugs came over and asked for money from him for our company's 'protection.' He refused, and they shot him dead."

Suddenly, so many furiously converging thoughts consumed me. I imagined her children's lives turned upside down and wondered about the difficulty that came with the loss of their father. I wondered about Kathy and, in a strange way, felt her pain: decisions about her home, her business, her children, herself...her *everything*. Tears ran down my face. She stopped me and said, "No, no, no, it's okay. That's just *part* of the story."

I listened.

"Months before his passing, a couple of guys had come by to try to sell us life insurance. Each night for about a week, my husband and I argued about the idea of purchasing life insurance. I was against it. What good reason was there to buy it? We were young. We were strong. We were doing well. We had a successful business, a nice home, and two beautiful, happy, and healthy children. Nothing bad could or would happen to us! Why in the world would we ever spend our money on something we'd have to die to benefit from?

"The subject seemed to slip away until one morning, when he softly told me, *'Kathy, you don't need to get any, but I'm going to buy some of that life insurance. I haven't been able to sleep. I keep thinking about the kind of father and husband I'd be if tomorrow didn't come for me and I left you and the family I love so very much financially unprepared.'*

"He didn't buy as much as they recommended. But you know, when all was said and done, that life insurance saved my life. It allowed me to freely pay the bills without even taking a moment to think about them. It allowed our business to carry on and for me to take my time to ultimately find the right buyer at the right price for it. It allowed me to keep my home and to be with my children. It gave me time to grieve and to decide what I might do next in life. *It saved my life.*

"I constantly hear you questioning the life insurance companies, their products, and the people that sell them, yet those products saved my life, and the people that sold it to us are now heroes in my life.

"Your family represents the heroes in my life, Stephen. And you, who question the companies, their products, and the people that sell them, need to stay in the business to protect us—the people like me who depend on them."

The very next day found me doing what I needed to obtain my license to sell life insurance in California. I was on a mission to find every single mother I could help. Suddenly, I was committed. Kathy's story and a slew of unanswered questions kept weighing on me: *What would happen if Kathy passed away? Where would her children go and what would they do? Who would take care of them? Would it be their grandparents, an aunt or uncle, or someone else? Who would finance their care?*

People die. *Everyone* dies. Life insurance death benefits provide survivors with cash when their loved one passes away. This money helps them address financial issues that could cause undesired problems for them at a time when they're dealing with many *other* emotions and they don't need financial woes added to the mix.

Hannah, the teacher who was struggling with her new position as a life insurance consultant, never understood the honor of helping a person in this way. She didn't understand that, as a financial advisor, she could do good in the world for people who need it and are at the lowest points in their lives. She didn't understand the value of what we do.

I don't blame Hannah for this misunderstanding. She was never taught the value of what she was providing. Like most salespeople, she was focused on learning how to sell products. I was fortunate to meet Kathy and experience the value of what financial advisors do early in my career and was happy to have the opportunity to share the lessons it taught me with Hannah.

## THE DICHOTOMY OF TRADITIONAL FINANCIAL ADVISING

Initially, most advisors are trained to sell products. They then learn to broaden their expertise and effectively present sales concepts. Some evolve into financial needs analysis experts. Others rely upon consultative processes driven by leading questions. Still others—a rarer breed—become holistic planners who bring together many areas of expertise to serve their clients. In the end, despite the best initial intentions of advisors, most techniques purposefully work toward influencing prospects to take actions motivated by fear. Advisors continue to sell in this manner because they're powerful and effective methods for closing deals.

We find ways to convince ourselves that what we're doing is the very best for our clients. How could it be otherwise? It's working—they're buying—right? This belief begins to entrench itself as we realize that we can't *always* provide what's best for people and over time, this belief becomes increasingly easy to accept. This is especially true as these techniques prove effective and result in financial success—for the advisor.

## INFLUENCE THROUGH FEAR

Fear is a powerful way to influence people, and many financial consultants find financial success for themselves by mastering their ability to position it as a key motivator. For example, an advisor hoping to sell long-term care insurance might position their message to make prospects believe that they're going to go broke and then become personally burdened taking care of their retired parents who become sick or disabled. A financial advisor may admonish a retiree to move their retirement funds away from their former employer and into investment alternatives that they represent instead to take better control over their financial future. Another might tell them they *need* life insurance to make sure their loved ones are cared for if they pass away while taking care of dependent kids who could never provide for themselves otherwise. While statements like these are true and may actually reflect the reality of the situation they're advising about, unless the advisor has all the facts of the situation and is acting in the person's best interest, they indeed represent the use of fear to drive sales.

## WE DON'T KNOW WHAT WE DON'T KNOW

Of course, this often means making a lot of assumptions. You assume that your prospects care about their parents or their kids and taking care of them above all their other cares. What if taking care of their parents isn't actually a prioritized concern of importance to them? What if they don't care about those things at all? Maybe their parents have their own insurance or dedicated funds for that concern. Maybe their relationship with their parents isn't very good. Maybe your prospect looks to the advice and counsel of the company-sponsored retirement plan provider. Maybe their plans allow for everything they want in retirement. They might have greater concerns than making sure their kids are left with a lot of money upon their demise. They might even have been previously denied coverage for life insurance.

If I bought every structured product that someone told me was the very best choice for me, I'd be totally invested if not broke by now. How did they know it was the best thing in the world for me? How could a product that is the best choice for me also be the best choice for everyone? It can't. Yet that's how many wealth advisors operate. They're focused on selling whatever they understand best, find of most value, or find easiest and most profitable to sell that day to put money in their pockets and satisfy their companies, at times with little to no regard for the clients (victims?) who bought from them.

## NO HARM, NO FOUL

Some advisors try to sell the company that they represent first, while others go right to selling a specific product that they find valuable or interesting to talk about. Other advisors believe they should sell themselves. Whatever their chosen methodology, financial advisors rarely believe they're doing harm to people.

We all believe we're doing good. That's certainly our intent. But when we're taught to focus on selling a product instead of focusing on the facts and hopes of the person we're selling the product to, are we living up to our good intentions? This creates a sort of dichotomy that's difficult to resolve in our minds: Are we helping or selling? Which is it?

On top of making those assumptions, selling this way doesn't necessarily respect people for who they are as individuals. Rather, it preys on their tendency to want to protect themselves from loss. People are much more afraid of losing what they have than they are inspired to chase something they don't have. They don't want to go broke taking care of their parents, and they don't want their kids to suffer because they didn't buy enough life insurance or save enough to live comfortably through retirement.

On the other side there's the promise of gain. That's another influencer—focusing on products and leading people to believe that they're going to earn higher returns in certain investments or be better off with that long-term care or life insurance policy they're recommending. It's easy for an advisor to convince themselves that what they're doing is the right thing to do, because, at times, they do just that.

Working for a company that operates under this pretext

presents the financial advisor with challenges. Perhaps your company requires you to sell certain products first and foremost. Maybe those they want sold first are products manufactured and offered by them. They may not necessarily care *how* you get it done; they will care that you *do* get it done and that you get it done through *them*.

In this traditional model, your company may encourage or even pressure you to start off by selling to your friends and family. They may remind you that "if they don't buy from you, they'll buy from someone else. They know and trust you—and you want to help them." This all sounds good, yet if you're not feeling good about what you're doing and how you're doing it, you'll be less inclined to contact the people you care most about to sell them on your company, your products, or yourself.

### BROKEN PROMISES

Whether you're a seasoned professional or just starting out, you toiled through exams, studied legal structures, and compared products and the like to become a financial advisor. There was a compelling reason. Perhaps you've forgotten what that reason was, so take a moment to think about it. Maybe a representative from a wealth management firm came to career day at your school or offered a free presentation at your local workforce center. Maybe you went to a job fair. Maybe a friend in a multilevel marketing organization strongly recruited you. However you got into it, it's likely the person who sold you on the idea made a lot of promises. You'd make a lot of money, for one. You'd be helping people while becoming rich beyond your wildest dreams and have a lot of free time. You'd be your own boss, make your own schedule, and call the shots in your career. It all sounded great.

If you've been in this business for three years or longer, congratulations. According to the expert data, you're among the 14 percent who succeeded, because 86 percent of aspiring financial advisors redirect their careers within the first three years of personal practice. That's something the representative at the career fair probably didn't tell you. And if you're at the bottom of that 14 percent, you're scraping by instead of living the life you were promised. You're not making a lot of money *or* having a great time doing it. You thought you'd be up there in the top 5-10 percent of those who "make it" in the financial planning industry. Instead, you're just surviving.

In addition to the money you expected to make and the life you thought you'd have, you believed you'd be helping people. You want to help people. Unless you're a sociopath, it's in your nature to help others. If you've done the work, gone through all the training, gotten all the right licenses, have access to the products and services people need to meet their goals, and are figuring out what those goals are, shouldn't it then follow that you're tremendously successful in this career? It should. You should be at the top of the heap, with people clamoring for your advice—and following it.

If you're not, there's a piece missing. Something's broken. The traditional way of financial planning often fails to deliver to what it promises.

## A NATURAL PIVOT POINT

A lot of advisors don't feel right about what they do, and they don't understand why they feel the way they do. Perhaps it's because they've yet to see the good that's possible. They don't yet realize that when you change the way you feel about people and how you work with them, you can feel great about what you're doing and how you're doing it.

When I work with new people at my company, I hear stories that remind me how prevalent the traditional approach to advising is and how unhappy many of the people are who are caught up in it. These stories are all too often the reality for those who choose to be a consultant of financial services products. Traditional financial advising misses the mark for the advisor and leads them to feeling unsatisfied about what they're doing and how they're doing it.

During training classes I'm often told, "This isn't how I've been trained to do this at other companies. All these years I've been focused on trying to sell a certain product from a certain organization. I've been talking about how many years the company's been around and how you can trust it. I talk about the services we provide and how many people we serve. I talk about the bells and whistles of the product I'm supposed to sell and do my best to convince them that they need it. You aren't saying any of those things. You ask them what was important enough for them to come to see you, and you focus on them. *No one preaches that.*"

I do believe that other advisors share my beliefs and intentionally focus on the clients who seek their guidance, but this approach isn't as common as it should be. I can't control how other advisors operate; I can only control my own actions, and I know what I do. I seek to learn why they're with me and ask prospects, "What was important enough to motivate you to see me today?" They tell me what they're concerned about, and I ask them what's important about what they're concerned about to them, and they keep talking. It's great conversation as I help them discover and share what they desire for their lives. I seek to understand those I wish to help plan to take better control over their futures. I do not seek to get them to understand what I sell, at least not initially. Frankly, they don't usually care about what I have to sell. They care about their lives and the way they hope to live them.

Another advisor colleague told me he had been with another company for six months, and after joining my company, it took him six months to unlearn lessons learned at his former place of employment. I discouraged his thoughts of "unlearning" and instead encouraged him to consider his experience a natural point from which to pivot and evolve on his journey toward becoming the financial advisor he aspired to be. And that's exactly what he did. As he put it, this new way of being a financial advisor "became a part of me."

Advisors want to do the right things for the people they serve. We want to ensure the products and services we provide play a role in getting our clients what they wish for in life. Traditional practices don't always allow for that to happen.

For me, this is where Ohana and Mahalo come into play—treating people like family and having gratitude and appreciation for everything in life, including those prospects we hope to convert to becoming our clients. Think about how approaching people as Ohana and with Mahalo changes the dynamic between you and others. Instead of seeing prospects as targets, you see them as the people you care about most in life. And if you actually are taking on your friends and family members as clients, isn't this how you want to treat them anyway? Isn't this how you want to treat all the people of importance in your life? Be grateful for the opportunity to meet these people and appreciate them enough to seek to understand what's of importance to them.

You can do things differently. You can change. The extent to which you're able to master a new way of doing good to do better for your clients can ultimately define your professional success and your personal fulfillment.

This is how you close the gap between what you're doing for clients and what you truly believe you should be doing for them. When you take the "selling" out of it and focus on the person, that gap dissolves. You're helping a person achieve their objectives, and the "buying" just *happens*. This is what separates traditional financial advising from Aloha financial advising.

## BREAKING AWAY FROM THE PACK

Once I began focusing on the person and stopped thinking about myself, my career changed. The dynamic between me and my clients changed, and I began to really enjoy them. I looked forward to meeting with them. It wasn't perfect at first. At times, I'd go back to the shark mentality: someone would talk to me about something they believed they needed, and my mind would immediately jump to a product I could sell them to fit that need. I'd jump in with the sale, and *bingo*—I'd jeopardize my chances to close the deal. Sometimes I'd lose the prospect. When I did succeed to close the sale in this way, rarely did my customer become a lifetime client, much less an advocate for me and my practice.

My company suffered a downturn on the tail end of the Global Financial Crisis of 2008. After sixteen years of sustained annual 31 percent growth, we hit a rough spot. It was like going off a cliff, with zero new revenue for eighteen months. I had about one hundred people on payroll and a host of expenses that relentlessly continued. When that happens to you and your business, you feel yourself caught up in a death spiral with no way to crawl out. That's when the shark mentality takes over, and even preachers like me who know better find themselves resorting to the old tactics we initially relied on to survive.

That's what I did. I lost sight of what led to the success I enjoyed in the first place, and whenever I saw an opportunity to sell something, I jumped all over it. Things got worse and worse, and deep down, I knew why. I knew I had to stop. I was ashamed. It was sickening. To recover, I had to consciously remind myself, "This is not who you are, Stephen." And it wasn't. I had to refocus my vision on what others cared about—those I pledged to serve—and find the courage to break away from the pack, advisors who were doing whatever was necessary to make the sale. Once I successfully did that, business quickly returned.

I recovered and so did my company. That didn't happen on its own—I had to stop worrying about poor, poor, pitiful me and reconnect with people's hopes and dreams, what they found of most importance to make their desired reality, and focus on ensuring that the recommendations I gave them were aimed at doing so. I had to ground myself and return to my reasons for embracing this profession. I had to remember what I was doing and why I was doing it and be there for others, not for myself. Doing that saved my company, and I know that any financial advisor who feels desperate at times, or like they need to make every sale that presents itself, can succeed if they make the shift and focus on those sitting across from them rather than themselves.

I also credit my key employees with the company's recovery. They always believed in why we were doing what we were doing. They stood by our mission and never wavered. These people who I worked with every day were a constant reminder of what we were about, and why we did what we did. They placed their unquestioned trust in me and all that I believed in, and they insisted we continue on that path. They are the real heroes of that chapter in my life.

It's easy to get drawn away from Aloha financial advising, especially if you have a prospect ready to make a large investment or you feel desperate to make a sale. You must dig to find the courage to be true to who you are and fight the urge to jump prematurely to the sale. Remember that once you establish your own core values and make a commitment to them, they should inform your client experience. Trust them to direct you.

### KŪLIA I KA NU'U

*Kūlia I Ka Nu'u* was the motto of Hawaii's Queen Kapiʻolani, who encouraged people to "strive to reach the summit." The summit is your personal best—your own version of excellence. As you read each chapter in this book, take a moment for self-reflection and to think about what you can do today to become your best version of a values-based Aloha Advisor.

It's not easy to let go of the mentality that comes with the traditional financial advising model. It's up to you to make the change, and you *can* do it. You can pivot toward a new way of financial advising. The results will come slowly, and when they do, you'll be amazed by the transformation and the results.

These are lessons I teach other advisors, and they're what I talked to Hannah about. She could connect with her prospects and learn to value what she had to offer. She could break away from the pack and be a financial advisor who listened to people's hopes and dreams, instead of just selling them her company, her product, or herself.

The key takeaway to break the routine of traditional selling is to start connecting with people. Discover their hopes and dreams. That's what I did, and it saved my career.

Seek to learn, understand, and appreciate people without judgment. Consider how your choices—what you choose to ask, discuss, and encourage your prospects to do—affect how you feel about what you're doing for them. Learn about their real and personal concerns instead of making up stories and potential circumstances to scare them. Know that life is scary enough, and you can help people prepare for whatever comes their way. What you offer as a financial advisor is of great value, especially when you first learn to value the people you serve and seek to do your best for them.

Do this today, on your next call. Tune into the person in front of you and seek to understand them. Afterward, think about how you feel about that person and more importantly, about yourself. Are you beginning to understand how valuable you can be to others? As an Aloha Advisor, you can feel like that every day.

# HOW TRADITIONAL WEALTH MANAGEMENT MISSES THE MARK FOR CLIENTS

Years ago, Swiss banks began selling US dollar denominated life insurance policy "packages" backed by US dollar timed deposits or other dollar savings plans and Japanese yen-based financing. You might still find variations offered by private bankers across Hong Kong and Singapore. This structured set of products was initially created in response to the extremely large income and inheritance taxes that many ultra-high net worth people face as they transfer their wealth from one generation to the next. These packages come with a lot of fees and commissions for the loans, bank accounts, life insurance policies, timed deposits, and other investments required to put them together. They're sexy-looking packages, financial advisors like them, and they sell very well.

To me, the package seemed strange because the products all focused on lifetime issues rather than on providing the large death benefits needed to pay the wealth transfer taxes these structures were originally intended to address. I learned that one reason for this was cultural: policies in certain parts of Asia, where the societal expectation is to spread your wealth, were structured on morbidity, not on mortality. There, lifetime benefits make sense and are generally what the people expect. As for me, I'm more accustomed to utilizing certain policies in the United States, designed to pay the taxes due and protect a person's wealth so it could be passed on with significant death benefits. These are the types of life insurance policies we use to create the liquidity we need to pay our wealth transfer taxes in the United States.

There were also a number of moving parts. A US dollar account earning much more than yen-based LIBOR (London Interbank Offered Rate) financing was a perfect strategy when US dollar interest was robust and yen financing rates minimal. A US dollar account, underlying US dollar-based cash value account and US dollar-based death benefit, works well when the US dollar strengthens against its yen counterpart. When these structured plans were first established and sold, the economy of the world perfectly set the stage to inspire dramatically valuable results. Advisors couldn't resist selling them and the wealthy couldn't resist buying them. This was especially true for people from countries who rely heavily upon bank financing to help them with their personal and business growth.

Over time, the world economy changed, as it always does. Currencies and interest rates fluctuated, and the dynamic between US and Asian economies shifted. As this dynamic shifted, so did the overall effectiveness of these packages. They were no longer suitable for the people who had purchased them. They began to fall apart.

The financial advisors who sold these packages were focused on the products' immediate sex appeal and relative compensation instead of on their clients' long-term expectations and hope and market realities. The lesson here is that when you sell something simply because it's attractive to you, you're probably selling it for the wrong reason. Basically, you're selling it to yourself.

Some of the people who purchased these packages came to me and my company for help. In some cases, the involved plans were structured quite conservatively. Even those structured in fairly conservative form found themselves underwater and in need of being bailed out. Less than 25 percent of the packages were salvageable, much less profitable for the people who invested in them.

By the way, where did the people who sold these packages—the advisors—go? Why didn't they follow up with their customers when things started to change for the worse? Being an advisor is easy when everything's going well. Aloha Advisors stand by their clients through the challenges, too. That's when they're needed the most.

## A SEXY PACKAGE THAT QUICKLY LOSES ITS SEX APPEAL

Plans that rely on elements of a particular economy only work while the economy remains the same, and that is never the case. Amazingly, packages like the one I described are still being created by different banks and insurers, because financial advisors find them intriguing and profitable to sell. It's also because the economics will once again lean toward promises of success. This is the case even though investors, and even at times advisors, don't always thoroughly understand them or all the variables and risks involved in these packages—variables and risks due to the reality that, in life, things are rarely constant and are subject to change.

I see this happen time and again in the financial world. These packages are often structured products of greed, not need. On the surface they can look like the cure-all to every financial woe and the direct line to certain prosperity. Usually they aren't the panacea that they're marketed to be, though they can make the bank and the financial advisor a lot of money while providing less than what people truly need to satisfy their wants.

There is a caveat to this, because sometimes packages like this work well. Sometimes they make perfect sense to place within a person's financial portfolio. Unless the representing financial advisor understands its components, benefits, and relative risks, and can clearly communicate this to their prospect, one potentially wades in danger of providing an offering that fails to serve the individual.

Ultimately, financial products are nothing more than a place to put your money so it's there and maximized for you in certain situations. It's nothing more than that, and you shouldn't kid yourself or anyone else into thinking that it is. It's their life that matters, not whether you sell a product. It's their goals that matter, not yours. When I remove my personal goals and opinions from the mix and focus on my clients, I maximize my ability to call on and provide the professional acumen required to help them get closer to what they wish for in life. Anything less is an obstacle in the process of successful financial advising.

## EDUCATION IS KEY

My team and I spend a lot of time educating advisors and learning from them, too. We meet with other investment advisors, insurance advisors, general financial advisors, tax advisors, legal advisors, and other experts with whom we collaborate to ensure a full understanding of involved legal structures, the products and services that go behind them, the lifetime tax consequences, and, most importantly, the total result. We must ensure that those we partner with understand the value and the risk of each type of offering to avoid promoting anything that detracts from catering to their and our shared clients' desires.

This follows the core value Imua. Continuously seek to learn, grow, and become more valuable to other advisors, your clients, and theirs by doing so. Treat people like family, Ohana, and help them confront the reality that some policies or structured products may seem attractive and are therefore easy for you to sell yet may fail to serve their best interests.

Examples of wealth management products that make sense for some and not for others include captive management arrangements, reverse mortgages, private placement investments or insurance products, home equity loans, real estate investing, life settlements, and infinite banking, where money is invested in cash value life insurance policies, hedge funds, and so on. The list goes on forever. Virtually all financial products vary in their ultimate value to any one particular person.

It's up to us as advisors to make the right recommendations to our prospects and clients. Depending on a person's situation and hoped for outcome, these may represent meaningful options. But unless we fully understand the variables around these products, and unless we act as caring expert professionals, we might simply recommend a product that's not properly fit for them. Generally, financial products in and of themselves are meaningful. Yet if applied in the wrong way with the wrong person under the wrong circumstances, the outcome may be less desirable, even disastrous.

The bottom line is that the best plan is the one that provides whatever the people who look to you for guidance *need* in order to get what they *want*. People desire different things for different reasons, so it's imperative to look at every one of them individually. Stop looking at products and spending precious time to figure out how they might fit, and instead look at the situation and goal, figure out what clients seek, and determine what they need to get it. This is the mindset shift that's required for you to stop missing the mark.

## WHY THIS PROBLEM PERSISTS

Insurance and investment products continue to be inappropriately sold because the advisor either (1) doesn't understand the product or (2) does understand it and sells it anyway, even though it's not the best product for the person's plan. They say that when the only thing you have to work with is a hammer, everything looks like a nail. That product that we're so enamored with becomes the answer to all, even when it isn't.

In chapter 2, I talked about how traditional financial advising methods and the mentality around them contribute to advisors' failing to do good for their clients. There are other reasons for why this happens. Sometimes advisors sell because they think the product is clever or cool—whoever designed it has figured out a smart way to make money. The advisor might not consider the sustainability of the product, or its suitability: how it fits desired outcomes.

There's also a greed factor here: it's tempting to sell something exotic and large all while earning the highest of commissions. Recall the dichotomy of traditional financial advising presented in the previous chapter. Are you helping, or are you selling? Advisors might justify a bad selling decision in their minds by insisting that the strategy is amazing when all factors come together and better than nothing at all, regardless of how the future economy pans out. Is that really serving the person's best interests?

People continue to buy because they don't know any better. They're told the investment is the best thing out there and since they've got money sitting idle, not doing anything for them, why shouldn't they put it to work? Frankly, there's a lot of truth in that thought.

The problem is compounded when an advisor convinces their newly sold clients to tell everyone they know and care about to buy whatever it is that was sold to them. People listen to recommendations from their family and friends. How many times have you worked with someone who had made terrible choices in their portfolios based on the advice of a nonexpert? They purchased this or that policy or investment because their brother has it or their cousin recommended it.

If you ask them, "What was important about what that investment did for you?" they usually don't know or can't remember. They haven't had the rational thought process tied to conversations that discover what they want, and the odds that this thing they put their money into will give them what they need to get there are slim.

Call it "fear of missing out" (FOMO). Call it the little red Corvette syndrome, where it's fun to imagine yourself driving around town in a sporty little number, even though your car insurance is going to go up and your odds of getting pulled over are going to go *way* up. We aren't thinking about speeding tickets when we make the purchase—we're thinking about zooming down the freeway with the top down and the wind in our hair. We're thinking of the flashy car everyone else is driving and how we don't want to be the only one on the block who doesn't have one.

Buying decisions are emotionally driven, and you know this. Your clients, on the other hand, may not be aware that emotions can lead them to make poor financial decisions. Sometimes you need to stop them from doing so.

### BACK TO OHANA

Selling people what you think is cool or filling an order for products that your prospects think are cool can lead to undesired consequences. They may not get what they're looking for and what they trusted you to deliver.

If you approach your position with a strong moral compass, with Pono, the goal of doing right, the odds of advising them in a way that satisfies their desired outcome increases dramatically. Remember Ohana, the value of treating people like family and sometimes telling them things they need to hear for their own good. This is sometimes what's required when your prospects want to buy something that isn't necessarily a good fit.

You don't have to do this, by the way. There is no imperative that says you have to do your best for the people you serve, and it's possible (and likely) that if you don't meet their wants 100 percent, you still won't put them in a terrible situation. If you think that's good enough, then that's your decision to make. That doesn't work for me.

If instead you focus your attention on doing the best for people as their lead advisor, you'll find that it doesn't take much more effort to properly direct or redirect their cash flow and encourage the garnering of proper assets and proper placement of those assets in their portfolios in a way that fulfills their optimum desired outcome.

Advisors must sometimes separate themselves from their organization's portfolio of product offerings to do this. Unless they're specialists who are expected to do so, advisors can't live and die by a premade financial investment, insurance, or wealth management package. People are unique, and their wants are unique. Focusing on products to sell rather than the situation of the person in front of you may lead you to miss the opportunity to achieve your goal of becoming your clients' trusted total wealth advisor, an Aloha Advisor.

## THE NEW TRANSPARENCY

The financial world never ceases to change. Today there is much more transparent information on financial products and investments readily available to the public. People don't have to make decisions on blind trust. They can educate themselves and find out if what you're telling them is true. Is what you're selling them what they need to help them get what they want?

If it's not, they'll question your reasons. Why put yourself in that compromising situation? If you instead make the effort to learn more about your prospect and find the proper strategy and ideal array of products and services for their situation, you'll win every time. With practice, you can improve your conversation skills and your ability to match people with the right products and services. Each time you meet with them, you'll know more and be more prepared, and you'll be able to do better for them every time.

Imagine how much more powerful you can be as an advisor with this ability. This is the essence of how you go from closing 20-30 percent of your cases to creating lasting relationships with nearly everyone who engages with you.

## LEARN TO LISTEN

Your first responsibility to people who seek your counsel is figuring out where they want to go in their lives, and your second responsibility is learning where they are relative to where they want to go. What's important about how they enjoy their retirement to them? What's important about the kind of legacy they leave behind to them? Be truly interested in people and accomplish this important task. Learn to be a good listener.

I learned the power of being a good listener by accident. I was looking forward to a first date lunch with a beautiful young lady when I developed this huge pimple on my face. I could feel it throbbing on my nose and I was mortified, not knowing what to do. At lunch, I barely spoke for fear that my pimple would pop. This girl talked and talked and talked through the entire lunch. I sat there, nodding my head now and then and paraphrasing her words back to her to let her know I was listening and understood her. I may have even seemed interested. I was not. Actually, I was thrilled when the check finally came!

Surprisingly, the girl gushed about what a wonderful time she had. She wanted to know what I was doing that weekend. At first, I didn't understand why she liked me so much. I had barely uttered a word during our time together. Then I realized: it didn't matter. I listened, and she felt heard. And, because I nodded and repeated what she was saying, she felt understood. She felt safe enough to trust me and wanted to spend time with me. Funny thing: I don't know if she even noticed my enormous pimple!

If you care about people and listen to their stories, they'll keep sharing more and more with you. The more they talk, the closer you'll get to wherever it is they want to go. Along the way, they'll begin to trust you because you're listening and seeking to understand them. You're not judging. You're not focused on your opinion or limited by your biases—you're only trying to learn theirs—and this makes them feel appreciated and understood.

People want to be heard and not judged. They want to be understood. They want to tell someone about their hopes and their worries and their dreams and their fears. The more you seek to understand these things about your clients, the more you will understand, and the more trusting dynamic you'll achieve with those who seek your counsel and guidance.

Focusing on your product is the obstacle that gets in the way of that happening. Your prospects need to feel understood before they can trust you enough to allow you to guide them.

## KEEP AN OPEN HEART AND A QUIET MIND

When I speak with prospects and clients, I keep this in mind: *keep an open heart and a quiet mind.* "Keep an open heart" means to listen with Aloha and Mahalo, love and gratitude. Take in this person's views, opinions, cares, judgments and hopes and all that's of importance to them. Just *listen.* "Keep a quiet mind" means to respond to their words with Pono and Imua. This means not allowing my personal biases, opinions, or judgments to interfere with my thinking. With Pono, I seek to do the right thing by this person; with Imua, I learn to understand them, even when we do not agree.

This takes time to master. We're used to letting our biases affect the stories we hear. We're used to thinking too much about what we care about instead of considering what others care about. Our experiences, thoughts, and ideas like to raise their voices. Unless the story we hear is exactly like ours, we don't see it for all its beauty. How often is another person's story exactly like mine? Never. We seem so similar on the surface and we can be so different at the core. So I train myself to keep an open heart and a quiet mind when I meet with people.

If someone asks for my personal opinion, I'll share it. When I do, I always remind them that they've asked for my personal opinion and it's not my professional opinion that I offer. If they need to hear my professional opinion on something they're considering, I'll share it only after I've heard them out and fully understand what they desire in life. If I tell them my opinion without understanding that, then what I share may provide little in value to them, as it's simply my personal opinion and what may apply to me and not an opinion that applies to them. My professional opinion should always be based upon their facts and realities and what's important to them, not on my facts and realities and what's important to me.

I also remind myself that we're all different. No one is 100 percent right, and no one is 100 percent wrong. We are each unique, and we may have overlapping opinions on some things. Yet it's not likely that any of us will ever agree 100 percent with another person 100 percent of the time. That's OK. It's helpful to be open to that and appreciate others for who they are.

One of my favorite quotes comes from author Tony Alessandra. He said, "Treat others the way they want to be treated." This Platinum Rule, as he calls it, is different from the Golden Rule, which suggests you should treat people the way *you* want to be treated. The Platinum Rule puts the wishes of the other person ahead of your own and aligns with how I aspire to treat my prospects and clients.

## PREPARE FOR THEM, NOT FOR YOURSELF

We're told what we're supposed to sell and how we're supposed to sell it. At the end of the day, what's most important is finding out what matters to the people we serve. Discover what's important to them and let go of everything else that you know.

When I began my career in financial advising, proper preparation for every meeting was everything. I had to have the right portfolio of materials and array of products and the right legal forms, and I had to understand all the tax codes, regulations, and more.

I still believe in being prepared, and I study constantly to keep up with those things. Bringing a lot of materials to an initial meeting, however, isn't necessary or even important to me today. If a prospect says they want specific information on a specific product or topic, of course I show up prepared to discuss it with them. Still, I don't prepare the way I used to. I don't show up for an initial meeting with the intention of necessarily presenting a prearranged set of sales concepts or selling them any specific product.

Today, my preparation is much simpler. I take a moment to tell myself why I'm meeting with this prospect. You can call it a prayer, or a meditation, or anything you like. Basically, it's a reminder to myself that this isn't about me. With Mahalo, I know I'm sincerely blessed with the opportunity to meet this unique person and learn of the life they seek, and I ask for the strength and the resolve to know that the true guide of how I may add value is within the person in front of me. Their lives, and what's important to them, will guide us to the right answer for that person.

Nothing in our conversation will be important to me unless it's important to them. The only importance I bring exists if it delivers something of importance to them.

## KŪLIA I KA NU'U

Preparing this way takes very little time. Still, you must train yourself to do it, and you'll need much practice to do it well.

This method works anywhere, anytime, and anyplace in the world. Try it for your next call with a prospect. The first time you do, feel free to bring everything you typically would and leave it all in your briefcase. Let a notepad and pen be your tools, along with your eyes, ears, questions, and your attention to the person in front of you. Be intentionally present for them. They'll tell you everything you need to know.

# A DYNAMIC BUILT ON TRUST BETWEEN YOU AND YOUR CLIENTS

My father, a third-generation American of Japanese ancestry and second generation in my family in the insurance and investments business, ran what is called a "master agency," an organization recognized for producing at a particularly high level among other agencies across the country. He wanted to discover the secrets of his firm's top performers, so he invited them to spend a couple of days together, primarily sitting around a table (maybe enjoying too much scotch) and sharing their best practices. I was the newest guy in the group.

After two days of discussion, my father came to the conclusion that the only difference between his top financial advisors and those who were not *quite* as good amounted to just two things: (1) the high performers were more strategic in their thinking and in their work style, reflected in their committed work ethic above and beyond that of their counterparts, and

(2) they carried personalities that allowed them to connect better with others.

Based on those findings, my father decided that the people in his firm who weren't top performers simply needed to work harder and more strategically and improve their communication skills. No doubt, hard work and being able to connect with people go a long way in almost any job.

I bought it—at first. *Could it be that simple?* And if it is that simple, then how can I work more strategically and what can I do to communicate better? I knew *I* was doing something specific, and it wasn't just about hard work and rapport. My prospects and clients seemed to sincerely *trust* me, and the relationships we shared made my work much more enjoyable. I thought about how I made that happen, and that's when I discovered another secret—one I hadn't learned over scotch.

## BUILDING TRUST INTENTIONALLY

I wasn't always a fan of constant and proactive learning. It wasn't until I found my calling to serve others in the financial planning industry that I embraced the spirit of Imua, of moving forward and doing my best. Since then, I've become a lifelong learner. I read books and articles, attend seminars, and seek out mentors and experts to learn about various subjects that interest me or that might improve my professional skills. In my learning, I discovered Bill Bachrach's teachings and, specifically, his belief that trust can be built *on purpose.*

Bachrach wrote many books including *Values-Based Selling, Values-Based Financial Planning,* and with Norman Levine, *High Trust Leadership.* His system, referenced in the book

*Pearls of Wisdom II: How to Work with Executives* by Stephen Haines, proposes that you can intentionally create trust by asking questions that stir emotions. One of Bachrach's questions is *What's important about money to you?*

I knew from experience that prospects who trusted me became better clients who enjoyed better advice and counsel from me. They shared more and empowered me to do a better job for them. Borrowing from Bachrach's model, I began asking my prospects questions in the following way: *what's important about (fill in the blank) to you?*

This question shifts the focus away from products and toward whatever's on the person's mind right now. By asking questions formulated in that specific manner, I could uncover what was important to *them* instead of focusing on what was important to me. My prospects began to open up to share their real thoughts and emotions with me. Asking questions in this manner almost always evoked the emotional connection I sought. *I had learned how to create a dynamic with people that was built on trust and to do so on purpose.*

My prospects and clients *wanted* to talk to me and tell me what was important to them. I simply needed to ask them properly phrased and positioned questions, and the more I asked, the more information they provided. As our conversations progressed, they began to discover *what was truly important to them that relied upon finances in the many parts of their lives*: family, friends, travel, retirement, and so on.

If I could help them dig deep by answering my questions, we could get to the core of their being and discover what made them tick, what they truly wished for in and out of life, and what nourished their souls. This is how I came to truly understand the person in front of me. I wanted to understand people so I could be the best advisor for them, and *they wanted to be understood.*

## SHARING ALOHA

Most advisors have what's called their "consultative process." I call mine "sharing Aloha." It's how I create a dynamic built on trust. Once I establish trust with prospects, we can move toward their goals around how they want to gather wealth, preserve it, and transfer it. A lot happens on the way to figuring out the best way to do that.

I put some structure around the conversation. I ask prospects what was on their mind and important enough to motivate them to see an advisor like me. People are busy, and meeting with a financial advisor takes both time and a whole lot of energy. They need to find space in their schedule, commit to it, and show up. Something must be very important for them to do that. They tell me why they're there. Maybe they want to review their pension plan, or they may have another advisor and they're just looking for a second opinion around the management of their wealth. Before we dive into a complete discovery, I explain what I do.

## WHAT I DO AND HOW I DO IT

You can't expect people who just met you to immediately and completely share their greatest hopes or personal facts and circumstances with you. I tell them that I want to hear more about why they came to see me and together we'll address those specific concerns. First, I want them to know what I do and how I do it. They need to know that they're talking to the right person before sharing their personal and deepest thoughts with me.

I share a little bit about what I believe are the fundamentals of financial planning. This isn't me talking about my company and how long it's been around, or about my products. It's simply to let them know how I generally approach financial planning. This logical conversation helps to set the stage and balance out the emotional conversation that follows. It also allows the individual to avoid feeling like they're expected to immediately tell me their life's history and confess their deepest thoughts. While it's vital to hear these things, people need to be at ease before they'll readily share their most treasured hopes with you.

I tell each prospect: "I promise to address in depth those issues you just mentioned that are of importance to you. Before I do, I'd like to first take a few minutes to let you know what I do and how I do it. I want you to understand my overall philosophy on wealth management and what I believe is fundamental toward securing a successful financial plan. Then you can decide if I'm a good fit for you. You wouldn't want to share a lot of information with someone who doesn't share your values, so let's get those out there now. Then you can decide if you'd like to move forward, and if you do, the rest of our conversation is going to be all about you and what's important to you."

People typically want to hear what I have to say along those lines at this stage anyway. Few are ready to move forward transparently without these assurances, and this helps us cut to the chase. The occasional exception involves prospects who come to me with a specific product in mind. They may be set on what they want and how much they want to spend on it. If this is their preference, we simply discuss the feasibility of the product. It's not my preferred way to work with prospects, but some people just want to buy something specific, and I won't simply turn them down unless it's an unsuitable choice for them. While I always strive to act in their best interest, I must also consider people's personal beliefs, and if they feel strongly about something, I must do my best to respect that, too. Furthermore, I've actually had customers formally complain when I didn't sell them a particular product that I was licensed to sell, even when I saw it as less than the best fit for them. I can only do my best to offer the most meaningful plans of action, and, ultimately, they write the check and make the final decisions as to which financial alternatives best suit them. If I've treated the situation with Pono, openly and honestly sharing my professional opinion on the matter as it relates to their stated goals and the product they desire securing, and whatever it is they wish to purchase won't serve to compromise their goals, I'll usually take the order. I've now got a new customer, and the next challenge will be converting them into a client and, ultimately, my advocate. That happens more often than you might imagine.

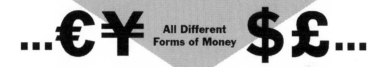

Savings, Certificates of Deposits (CDs), Loans, Hedge Funds, Asset Allocation, Stocks, Bonds, Commodities, Mutual Funds, Fixed Annuities, Variable Annuities, SPIA, IRA, 401(k), Deferred Compensation, Executive Bonus, Split Dollar, SRAP, Term Insurance, Whole Life Insurance, Universal Life Insurance, Second To Die Life Insurance, CRAT, CRUT, QDOT, Revocable Living Trust, Irrevocable Life Insurance Trust, Bank Accounts, Defined Benefit Plans, Money Market, Profit Sharing Plans, Hedge Funds, 529 Education Plan, Straddles, Mortgage, Puts, Calls, Gold, Bitcoin, Cryptocurrency...

**...€¥ All Different Forms of Money $£...**

| Banking | Investment | Insurance | Tax | Law |

# The Four Fundamentals of Financial Planning

❶ Make Money

❷ Wealth Accumulation

❸ Wealth Preservation

❹ Wealth Transfer

**Key: Position and reposition assets, direct and redirect cash flow to find better financial efficiencies in order to achieve client desired results.**

The fundamentals of Aloha Financial Planning.

Most prospects want to understand what I do and how I do it, though. I explain that there is an endless array of products in the financial world: 401(k)s, mutual funds, stocks and bonds,

IRAs, certificates of deposit, fire insurance, qualified plans, and so on. It can be daunting because there is so much. They all have one thing in common in that they're all different forms of money at the ready to address different things. Car insurance, for example, is money at the ready to fix damages or replace your car if you get into an accident. Fire insurance is money at the ready should your home catch on fire. Investments and insurance are all forms of cash that are at the ready for those times in your life that require an infusion of capital. These different forms of money are what financial advisors filter through for you in order to identify those that may offer value to you.

How you think about the different forms of cash can be simplified by arranging them into five categories: banking, insurance, investment, tax, and the law.

- **Banking** includes accounts to hold the money we require for daily living and loans that help us buy things we can't afford to pay for all at once.
- **Insurance** is money to protect those things we want or need in our lives—our homes, our vehicles, and our businesses. We insure ourselves and our ability to earn the income necessary to provide for the homes we live in, the vehicles we drive, and the businesses we own, too.
- **Investments** can deliver income you might need at some point in your life or instead grow for something you'll want in the future, such as a well-funded retirement plan, a legacy for charities, or a gift for your children.
- **The last two are closely related: proper legal structures that allow you to enjoy tax efficiencies.** This is where lawyers and tax advisors provide their expertise.

That's generally it, all that financial advisors like you and me need to consider when we're working with a prospect. These are the forms of cash that will ultimately help them get closer to what they want. It's our job to understand these things, not theirs.

I then explain that my job is to understand what they want regarding the four fundamentals of financial planning: (1) making money; (2) creating and building more wealth; (3) preserving that wealth; and (4) passing it on to the people and places they want it to go to during their life or upon their passing. How they make a living is up to them, but together, we can plan around fundamentals two, three, and four: wealth building, preservation, and transfer.

I let the person know that ultimately, we'll get them closer to their goals by directing or redirecting their cash flow and positioning or repositioning their assets to create better efficiencies for optimal financial results. Then I ask, "Does this make sense to you?"

This is a key moment in the consultative process, of when I'm sharing Aloha. I'm basically telling them that we'll be utilizing different strategies that may include investing in different products than what they currently hold to find these better results. Their positive answer indicates their potential willingness to allow me to place new products into their portfolio and that they're okay with accessing those insurance and investment instruments through me.

How we decide to do this, I continue, is based upon what's important about what happens to their assets in the context of what's important to them overall. We call this the discovery process, and I'll be asking many questions in order to truly understand them and what's important to them. Some of my questions may seem a bit unique and never have been asked of them before. It's important for us to ultimately figure out what it will take for them to be happy and fulfilled in their life.

I let my prospects know that once we understand all that they want, we'll need to know where they stand today relative to their hopeful destination. That is the time for us to collect the facts. My staff works with my prospects and clients to help them gather most of that. From there, we begin to look at where they stand relative to where they want to go. We consider adjustments and the role that banking, insurance, and investment products—along with taxes and the law—may further play in helping them. We take into account where they call home, too—and whether they're from the US, from another country, or multinational in scope. Our Idea Center evaluates all that information and provides thoughts and recommendations towards the design of plan alternatives that direct the client's cash flow and positions their assets to better align with their goals.

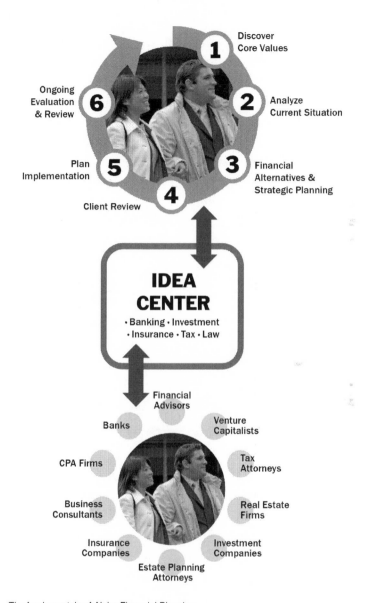

The fundamentals of Aloha Financial Planning.

Once I've reviewed the suggested financial strategies and
am satisfied that they prove of sincere value to the person, I

share those strategies with them, and, together, we decide which ideas make sense to prioritize and implement. We also identify those ideas that don't make sense and send them back to the drawing board, along with our feedback. Before I explain the plan in detail and how it satisfies their goals, I reconfirm what they desire in life. Whatever we recommend must address those things of most importance to them for their plans to work. This process ensures that my clients aren't receiving only what they thought they needed; they're getting what they truly need to address all their wishes.

At this point, I remind the person that financial planning is a lifetime concern and ours will be a long-term relationship. Life evolves, so expect us to regularly review all that's going on and adjust as their desires and realities in life dictate. Then I ask, "Shall we proceed?"

Their positive response sets the discovery process in motion, at which point I usually share how I get paid. I don't want untimely and undesired surprises, so I let them know that my one request is that, should they agree with my recommendations and plans of action, they implement elements of the plan through me. I've rarely experienced pushback.

## THE DISCOVERY PROCESS

Once the person understands what I do and how I do it and agrees to continue, and before my staff works with them to collect all the facts, I begin learning what's important to them through a discovery process. Their priorities might be related to creating, preserving, or transferring their wealth, and it may be for the benefit of their family, friends, charities, or their businesses. Each person takes me on their unique journey, and

I benefit from their amazing stories, their love for others, their life's work, and their hopeful life ahead. People are fascinating, and I'm grateful, full of Mahalo, to learn from them and about them. This is where the real sharing of Aloha happens.

You can't rush the sharing of Aloha. It's *always* a way of being that requires patience and persistence. It's vital to ask people questions and to continue to ask until you've exhausted their answers, or at least until they tell you "...and making all of that happen would make me so happy."

The conversation often turns to their assets. They may want to know how to better manage what they have or how to generate more. I can guide them to positioning and repositioning their assets and directing and redirecting their cash flow to help them do so. But first, I need to understand what ultimately matters to them so that we can make the right decisions to get them to direct and redirect into strategies that will effectively lead them to what they truly want. We need to talk through all of it in order to get to what it is that will make this person happy.

A person might tell me that they wish to speak with me about their retirement. So I ask, *what's important about what happens in your retirement to you?*

From there, they might tell me that they want enough money in retirement to live comfortably, or to travel, or to have a second vacation home. Then, I dig deeper along each of those areas: *tell me, what's important about having that second vacation home in retirement to you?* I do my best to minimize my assumptions because what people want within these matters is uniquely theirs. It's critical to understand what the person in front of me wants and what's important about these things to this person.

Sometimes the person I'm listening to has made assumptions, too. They might tell me that they need retirement income starting at age sixty-five yet have no real reason for choosing that retirement age. When we dig, we might learn that they love what they do and may actually want to work longer, or they may want their retirement savings to last longer; in either case, it may be wise to consider a different retirement age, one that makes sense for them. Our conversations flush out all those assumptions so we can work together from a place of truth.

I didn't learn this in my initial advisory training. Like many of you, I was taught to sell products, the company I represented, and myself. I was also taught that most people needed to hear the same things, as they cared for the same things. While we certainly share similar hopes, we're far from being the same. To sincerely connect with people, it was imperative for me to put those teachings aside and focus on understanding each person. I had to appreciate what was important to them and do so without judgment. This is easy when you agree with people and you're aligned with their beliefs. But when you're working with a person whose wants in life differ from yours, it's vital to seek to understand why they want what they want and appreciate what you learn regardless of your personal feelings.

For this, I enlist the core value of Aloha and approach people with open arms and with love. This means that I approach every prospect and client with good intentions. I keep a quiet mind and do not judge them, and by not judging them with my open heart, my actions reflect that desire. I also resist any urge to offer a product or solution during the process of sharing Aloha. It may be too early in our discovery and doing so may lead them down an inappropriate path. This is where I call on my core value Pono. It's always best to counsel with righteousness to achieve the best and intended outcome.

Then, I confirm my understanding of what I understand to be of importance to them. Again, it's about my prospect, not about me. I repeat what I heard: "This, this, and this are important to you, and this is why they're important to you. This is what you want for these things in your life. Do I have that right?" They tell me more. They'll correct, confirm, and help shape the story until I understand them completely. Along the way, we learn to trust one another.

I give the person a summary of my understanding of what they want, why they want it, and where they are relative to getting it, along with the challenges they've faced that encouraged them to meet with me. Of the three—what, why, and how—the *why* is what makes it a priority for them. It's their inspiration, their purpose in life. When people are motivated by great inspiration, they find the will to power through the "what to do's" and "how to do's" to get there. As the late, great philosopher Friedrich Nietzsche stated, *"He who has a why to live for can bear almost any how."*

During this part of the conversation, people often tell me that they feel like they're reading a book about themselves. Even more surprising, they feel like they're reading it for the first time, and they're fascinated by what they've discovered. They see their lives laid out up to now, and as they talk about their desired outcomes, they begin to imagine how they might proactively and positively shape life ahead. Once I fully understand the person, I can present them with an initial document of alternate paths to help them get to where they want to go. They realize that they can act as architects if they choose to take control and do so. We discuss how we can make sure they're on track to get what they need to meet those outcomes.

The reactions I get from prospects after this experience are fantastic. It's a fantastic experience for me, too, and one I wish for all financial advisors. You literally feel them transition from your prospect to your client. It's not the feeling you get when you sell something. It's a feeling you get when you change a life. That's sharing Aloha.

## EXAMPLE OF A DISCOVERY

Receiving referrals is a high compliment, and I'm very happy when clients and advocates refer the people they respect and may even care most about to me. That was the case with a couple that was referred to me, Jake and Barbara.

Like all my first meetings, I began by asking them what was important enough for them to take time from their busy days to sit down with me. Then I briefly explained what I do and how I do it so they could get a feel for whether we'd be a good fit. This wasn't a long and labored discussion where I tried to sell them on me, my company, or any products. It was an introduction.

Then I told Jake and Barbara that we'd be focusing on what was important to them—and what they valued most. After we completed our initial discovery, my team would work with them to gather the information we needed to come up with a plan that gave them what *they* needed to get what they wanted, or at least closer to it. We may work with our Idea Center comprised of specialists across banking, insurance, tax, and the law to ensure the plan took into consideration the proper forms of money they'd need at specific times in their lives. Finally, I'd provide plans of action for them to consider, which we'd review at a future date and make adjustments so that everything they cared about would be taken into consideration and addressed in a manner most meaningful to them. Over time, we'd adjust as life called upon us to do so.

After explaining this process, I asked the couple if they had any questions or concerns about how I do what I do and if they found it agreeable. This is yet another key moment of importance in our relationship. While it's important to me that anyone I work with understands what we're doing and how we're going to do it, it's equally important to know whether a prospect agrees. Their agreement begins the real sharing of Aloha. Conversely, their disagreement usually signifies the end of our potential relationship together. In a matter of about fifteen minutes, you'll know if the person in front of you is sincerely a potential client who's worthy of you and your precious time. This is an amazing blessing when you consider the commitment necessary to properly prepare for the presentation of alternative financial paths, those ideas you wish to share that may or may not be appreciated by your prospects.

Then we began the real discovery. Since Jake had initially told me he wanted to make sure his family was properly cared for financially, I asked, "What's important about what your assets do for your family to you?"

When I ask questions of that nature, people often take a pause; they usually don't know how to answer right away. I give them time to digest and think about it, and if they don't respond, I let them know that their thoughtful pause is normal and that *most* people don't answer immediately. People are rarely asked questions like that by financial advisors and even less often ask these questions of themselves. The fact is everything materialistic that you and those who depend on you have in life is created—and limited—by the money you have.

Jake and Barbara agreed. So I asked, "Tell me what's important about what happens to these assets—which you've worked so hard to accumulate over time—to you?" They started talking about a new home they were thinking about buying, and how that purchase might affect their ability to put their son through college.

This opened a few doors into what this couple wanted, and I asked them more about their son, and discovered they had four children. All of them wanted to go to college, and some of them wanted to go to grad school. One was thinking of medical school.

At this point, I had to figure out what was more important to them—did they want to talk to me about getting another home or about sending their children to college? I had to know more.

After asking more questions, I learned that the second home was actually meant to replace their current home. They were thinking of downsizing, yet not until all of their kids were out of the house. I further learned their youngest child was just fifteen years old, so that gave us some context—a time frame to work with.

Between gifts from their parents and the funds they worked

hard to earn and diligently save since the birth of their first child, they were already prepared to fund for college. The reason they were looking to downsize was because once they became empty nesters, they planned to seek new experiences in their lives that they couldn't enjoy while taking care of four children. This was important to them. Whatever these new experiences might be—travel, events, learning new skills, whatever—was aspirational, and it was clear that they cared about it enough to make conscious decisions and commit to them to make their dream a reality.

This is the depth of understanding that you need to foster with your prospects to make them your clients. It's often not the first thing they tell you, or even the second or the third. Yes, the couple wanted another home, and yes, they wanted to put their children through college. What they truly desired was the financial freedom to fully enjoy their lives as empty nesters, and they needed a plan to make all of that happen.

I always ask one question at a time. The answer triggers my next question and leads me to move on to the next question. Slowly, I peel away the layers like you do with an artichoke to get to the heart of all they wish to accomplish. The conversation may be a little awkward or uncomfortable for you at first. You simply must keep to task and keep asking. Eventually, you'll find yourself wanting to ask even more questions than you initially struggled to ask. You realize that it's the best way to purposefully seek to clearly understand those you wish to help.

During these conversations, people often say, "I never knew I thought this way about my life. I didn't realize how strongly I felt about these things. I better think more about this and do something about it. Getting there would really make me happy."

The discovery process is an amazing gift when you separate it from fact finding. This is not what many traditional advisors do. Sure, there are many things to discover relative to the holdings a person has within their portfolio. As for me, there will be a proper time to do this, but sharing Aloha and the discovery process aimed at what's important to them at the core of their being must come first.

People are usually eager to work with me by this point. If I've done my job well, the plan we've come up with is all about them, and there's little reason for them to want to opt out of doing it. Of course, I've had a few people just wanting my advice with plans to implement with someone they know, such as a family member or friend who's in the business. This used to annoy me, because I'd spent all this time with them only for them to turn around and implement their plans through their cousin. Frankly, it still does. Then I'm reminded of my core value Pono and how I always seek to do things for the right reasons. Sure, I remind them of their original agreement to allow me to position assets and direct cash flow on their part. And, if I truly care about this person and my relationship with them, I won't let them just walk away and hope they get the help they need. I'm personally invested in them, spent energy to help them articulate their hopes, and created plans set for implementation that will lead to their happiness, and the best thing I can offer is a proper handoff to their chosen advisor. I ask them if I can review their plans with this person to ensure their understandings and share what products and services we believe are of value or required to implement the plan we've devised. I ask them if we can call this person right now.

Sometimes prospects are reluctant. In the end, they're usually happy to oblige me either in reconsidering and allowing me to follow through for them or in making the call to their chosen advisor. Though I want them as clients and believe I've earned my place as their lead advisor, I'm not trying to take business away from a trusted friend, and if that's who they really want to buy from, they should. They should buy from the person they trust, and sometimes there is another person in their lives who can offer everything I can offer and whom they trust more. By living and working with Pono and Aloha, I hope to inspire Mahalo, appreciation from them and, more importantly, live as the values-based advisor I aspire to be.

My father was right in believing that top advisors work harder. They're more strategic and are better at connecting with people, too. For me, establishing trust with people by doing everything I can to discover what's of most importance to them and to deliver to that end is what differentiates me from other advisors. My overall philosophy is that doing good for people means focusing on them, being interested in them for who they are, and caring about them enough to discover what they want out of life.

## CARING COMES FIRST

There's a saying—originally attributed to former US president Theodore Roosevelt—that's been repeated so often, it's become cliché, yet the truth behind it is unmistakable: "People don't care how much you know until they know how much you care."

Remember the days when salespeople sold vacuum cleaners door-to-door? Usually, when a person answered the door, they had little interest if any at all in the vacuum. But if they'd just had a party for their child, and cake and cookie crumbs covered the floor—*and* Grandma had thought it was a good idea to give the kid a new puppy that was tearing up everything in its path—well, now that vacuum looked pretty good! If the vacuum also cleaned carpets and swept up pet hair, it may look *great!* (Actually, in this case, a carpet shampooer would probably be an even better idea.) The salesperson didn't know what was going on inside the house. Wouldn't it have been amazing if they could walk down a street and know which houses needed a vacuum for pet hair, or for carpet stains, or for whatever else the vacuum they were selling did? Back then, the salesperson had no way of knowing what the situation was when they knocked on a door.

Financial advisors are in a similar situation. They can do something about it. By asking the right questions and remaining curious about people's situations, we can get a better understanding of what's going on in a person's life. The picture may not be 100 percent complete or perfect. Of course, it never really is as life keeps us on our toes, sometimes encouraging us to change our path. Regardless, we can aspire to create as vivid a picture as possible, instead of just trying to sell whatever's handy in our briefcase when we meet that person for the first time.

### KŪLIA I KA NU'U

If you want to know what it is that you have to offer people that they'll value, practice listening to them, learning from them, and finding out about their situation. I might have the coolest vacuum (or retirement investment, or life insurance policy, or real estate property) in the world. If it doesn't satisfy what the person sitting in front of me wants, it will be of little value to them.

Practice asking questions and listening to the responses. And review all your products and services—not for what they are but instead for what they do and how they provide value. Focusing on the person doesn't mean you have to forget about whatever it is that you represent. Whatever your clients want can be delivered, ultimately, with the right plan and supporting financial instruments—yours or someone else's. Since you know yours best, think about all the bells and whistles that make them special. These aren't add-ons that someone conjured up just to make more money—they're typically features that piqued a person's interest. They're extras that people see value in because they satisfy a need that meets a want that people have.

This isn't an exercise in connecting all your prospects' and clients' desires to all you represent. Regardless, you should understand how those things connect so that when the time comes to consider a plan, you have the knowledge to put something together that shows the person you're paying attention and heard them loud and clear when you discuss it with them.

# WHAT YOU NEED FROM CLIENTS TO BUILD TRUST

I've had too many experiences where prospects came to me soon after being mistreated by an insurance, investment, or financial planner. These people were angry. Some were rightfully furious. They had trusted their money to someone who was supposed to be looking out for them and instead took advantage of that trust.

At the end of these conversations, I'd say something like, "Thank you for sharing how poorly our industry takes care of the people we serve. It happens too often, and I'm sorry that your experience was what it was." To position myself with the chance to move forward productively, it's imperative for me to diffuse the situation. It's not easy to find the right words to say to an irate person. So I look to find words that let them know I understand and appreciate what they've said. Even though I had nothing to do with it, as a representative of the wealth management industry, I still feel partially responsible for their disappointing outcome.

## CLIENTS DON'T ALWAYS TRUST FINANCIAL ADVISORS

This chapter is about what you need from prospects and clients to create a dynamic built on trust. How do you do that when prospects have little reason to trust you, at least initially? They don't know you, and they may have had a horrible experience with another advisor or someone else from the world of financial planning and advising. They may question your credentials and your values.

Having a designation next to your name because you earned some industry certification or belong to a particular organization doesn't guarantee your trustworthiness. It doesn't mean you'll appropriately care for them or ask the right questions. It doesn't mean you have the products and services they need or that you'll be willing to collaborate with other advisors to fulfill their wants.

This makes the ongoing process of intentionally building trust critical to the relationships you build with prospects and clients. Trust isn't a given, and it's not automatic. Sometimes it never happens. If you're reading this book not as an advisor but rather as a person seeking financial advice and counsel, and you agree with everything in it, feel free to hand this to your prospective advisor and say, "This is what I want from you. Set the stage appropriately by telling me what you do and how you do it and then ask me about *me and what's important to me*. Don't tell me what product you represent and why I should buy it. Be interested in what I want and why I want it, and when I tell you, *listen*."

It's up to us to earn trust. Until a person receives us as their values-based, trusted advisor, we can't deliver to the best of our abilities.

So, as you know, I set the stage and focus on what's important to my prospects before asking for the facts or discussing options and alternatives. I also want the people I serve to investigate me. I want them to read up on me—check out my website and the reviews. Talk to people who have worked with me. Find out up front if I'm the kind of person they want to work with. I don't want to begin a relationship with cynicism—I want them to think "yes" or at least "maybe" when they come to see me, not "probably not." I want them to be prepared and at the ready to trust me to the extent that we can move forward with sharing Aloha.

## WITHOUT TRUST THERE CAN BE NO SHARING OF ALOHA

People who share Aloha with me give me the best chance to do my best for them. If they want me to do my best, they need to share freely. The more they share, the better the chances are to provide sincere value to them. When people trust you, they open themselves up to your informed influence. They believe that your motives and your counsel's intent are to help arm them with the proper information and tools to make the right decision for their circumstances.

Trust liberates and encourages people to openly share with you. This is what inspires them to tell you what they really wish for in life. Without earned trust, the chances are slim that they'll share all that they own and truly want, and you'll never be able to do your best for them. In the end, a lack of trust hurts the client more than anyone.

People should seek to do what's right for themselves. The onus is on advisors to build trusting relationships that afford prospects that opportunity. If the advisor veers from focusing on the person and instead goes right to selling a package, product, or service, that person should stop the interview. On the other hand, when advisors stay true to what their prospects care most about, they're wise to openly share their current financial situation and their hopeful future. They need to give more information—as much as they can. They need to continue sharing until their hearts and souls are clear and anything that's been holding them back is vacated. This is how they, and their advisor, will discover what's truly going to make them happy and allow them to carve a meaningful path to best get there.

## WHAT YOU NEED FROM YOUR CLIENTS

People who prejudge you and aren't willing to trust—perhaps due to previous negative experiences they've had—should consider the fact that advisors come in different shapes and sizes. Just because someone shares the same title as another doesn't mean they work in the same manner. It doesn't mean this new advisor is going to do whatever it is that their bad experience advisor previously did to them.

People usually bypass this urge to prejudge you if you reach out to them. The rather overused word "authentic" fits here. When you're authentic in your communication, people tend to respond favorably. Yet many advisors struggle with getting past the stigma they conjure in their own minds. They bring these beliefs to meetings with their prospects, and when they see that prejudgment frown on a prospect's face—the barrier of cynicism and distrust that goes up, the unwillingness to share openly—either they naturally begin to oversell because they believe they need to convince the person or they shut down. This is when it's vital for you to push yourself and prove that their beliefs about you, and about financial advisors in general, are incorrect. You *are* different. Indeed, you *can* be trusted. You're interested in them as people, and you want to help them.

An advisor came to me with this very issue. He felt that his prospects didn't trust him, and rather than meet their preconceived beliefs head on, he'd shut down. By doing this, he was proving to his prospects that he didn't care about them. I talked to him about how our behavior—and not our prospects'—is usually the real reason for our failure. This meant that he had the power to fix the problem. To do so, he needed to push through and lay the foundation for a trusting relationship. He needed to start asking the right questions in the right way. We practiced together—me as the judgmental prospect who thinks all advisors can't be trusted and him as the financial advisor who truly cares about people enough to find out what makes them happy. Over time he learned to break through the attitudes of his most difficult prospects to successfully create open and trusting relationships. He learned to stop taking things personally and to share with authenticity his own worries of how other financial advisors act to earn such negative perceptions, and he showed prospects that he was *just like them*—a regular person. More importantly, a regular person who cares about other people and is trying to make a positive difference in the world by serving others.

We can't control the actions and reactions of others. The only actions and reactions we can control are our own. Think about what you believe about yourself. If you believe you can't be trusted, you won't be. Perhaps you shouldn't be. And if this is the case, you really shouldn't be in this business. If you think you don't care about people and aren't interested in them, you won't be—and others will know it. If you're not getting the responses you want from people, you can't necessarily overtly change what they believe about you. You *can* change what you believe about yourself and project that positive change, and the chances are that they'll ultimately respond favorably to you. Of course, if you really don't care about people, please change your career and do so quickly. Thank you.

## AN EXERCISE IN HOW PEOPLE SEE YOU VS. HOW YOU SEE YOURSELF

Recently, I reached out to friends on LinkedIn. I've not been an avid user of that site, and I hadn't personally sent blanket messages out to contacts. I wanted to try something new, so I reached out to people individually to see if they or anyone they knew might want to help me expand my services. I asked them to help me locate the right people to help me share more of what I have to offer to others.

I was blown away by the response. Dozens of people replied to my message, asking me to contact them or directly referring me to a friend. Some people told me that they were glad I'd reached out to them and wondered why I hadn't done so sooner.

This made me question myself. Why hadn't I been reaching out to people to ask them to introduce others of like mind to me like this before? When it comes to my practice, I know that what I have to offer is of great value to anyone who needs it and is willing to give me a chance. So why hadn't I more forwardly offered my advisory services directly to people I knew? I pondered this for a while and finally concluded that I never fully recovered from my earlier shame around the tainted reputation that bad advisors imposed through their actions upon our industry. I feel good about what I do, but it's always been overshadowed by a history of financial advising that hasn't always been good for those who rely upon our advice and counsel and still isn't always ideal. I had allowed this fact to affect my confidence and define my reality. Upon realizing this, instead of hiding from it, I began to rage against it.

This experience also made me think more about the prospect's point of view. If they needed my help, why hadn't they asked me? In the case of friends, family, and close contacts, they knew I was trustworthy. They knew I cared and would do a good job for them. Still, they didn't reach out. I wondered if people have been conditioned to be sold. They know they want something and wait until it's offered to grab it. If this is true, then I needed to stop waiting for people to ask me for help and start asking for their permission to help them.

I could say here that I need prospects to ask me for my help. Of course, that would be ridiculous. I know that the stigma financial advisors have taken years to earn won't change in the minds of the public anytime soon. While I hope to help change that with this book and in my work, in the meantime, I believe it's up to me *and* you—those of us committed to doing good for those we serve—to promote what we do and do right by those who grant us the opportunity to provide counsel.

Financial advising deserves respect. If money were simply a commodity, I probably wouldn't feel that way. It's more than that. Money makes those things most critically important to a person a reality such as security, comfort, and quality of life. The financial advising profession is a respectable one when trustworthy people define it, and investors put their trust in those who do.

## TRUST GOES BOTH WAYS

Have you ever been cheated on? Do you remember how it made you feel? I remember the first time I knew that a girlfriend cheated on me. It was the worst feeling in the world. I was devastated, and once it happened, it changed our relationship. Worse, it affected my future relationships.

It's the same between an advisor and their clients. If you betray a person's trust, your relationship will never be the same. They won't trust you, and they may never completely trust another financial advisor again.

Here's the really strange thing: clients who don't trust you *may* break up with you, and they may *not*. That seems crazy, right? Think about it. Most people hate confrontation. They avoid it at all costs. When you confront someone about a betrayal, you acknowledge that it happened—and you must deal with the fact that you trusted someone and shared a lot of personal information with them only to find that person turn on you. This makes you feel vulnerable. It can be embarrassing, and the last thing you'll want is to make it worse. It's the same for your client. Rather than confront the "cheater," they often ignore the betrayal, at least for a while, and they won't be eager to share anymore. That's far from an ideal advisor-client relationship. No more Mahalo. No more gratitude. No more Aloha. No more love. The relationship may remain. But it will never be the same.

Betrayal comes in many forms, from sharing information

about people with other entities without their knowledge to introducing them to other advisors whom you have yet to fully vet yourself. You might try to justify betrayals by telling yourself you're acting in the other person's best interest. If you haven't disclosed your intentions and your actions to the prospect first, you're making assumptions about what they want. People usually want to maintain control over their own lives, and while they often need your guidance, the decisions they make regarding their finances must ultimately be their own.

Betrayals can be unintentional, too. Say you're an expert in one facet of wealth management and not in another, and you put together a plan that fails to address how the plan affects the prospect's taxes or legal situation. You may compromise their finances and inadvertently betray your already established trusting relationship as you implement it. Be aware of these things and seek to be thorough and transparent with all your dealings with people. Let them know when you're unable to advise them on certain matters such as those that pertain to the law or tax assessment. Better yet, align yourself with professionals who can ensure the results of a plan implementation lead to the goals you and your prospect seek and do so *before* you make a recommendation or begin that implementation.

Privacy is also a delicate issue in financial advising, in large part because so much information is readily available about people that wasn't in the past. There's a fine line between what you need to know and what's out there, and it's up to you to respect that line, no matter how fine it gets.

People have a right to hold advisors accountable. If an advisor betrays their trust, they should dump them. Then, they should find an advisor they *can* trust and do their best to let go of their previous poor experience instead of holding it against their newly chosen guide. They should vet the advisor carefully to ensure they're trustworthy, operate their practices by philosophies they find agreeable, maintain the proper skillset, and are supported by a team behind them that provides outstanding service and care. Once a trusting relationship is built, they should go all in and allow that advisor to give it *their* all to do the best job possible for them.

If you're working with prospects who are actively vetting other advisors, tell them to learn of their processes and beliefs. If the prospective advisor's answers prove less than satisfactory, advise the prospect to move on to another. If you have a prospect who's meeting with you for a "second opinion," find out why. Are they happy with their current advisor? Did that advisor betray their trust in some way? Learn what's important about seeking this second opinion to them. Regardless of the reason, they should stand confident knowing that their personal information and cares—their financial information as well as their very hopes and dreams—are being shared only with those they trust.

When people find that perfect advisor, it's ideal for them to refrain from cheating on *them*, too. Instead, honor the time and effort the advisor puts into them as valued clients to help them create a financial plan that leads to a life fulfilled.

We can't guarantee that everyone will respect what we do. Yet for us to do good for people in the long run, they need to stick with us and allow us to work with them throughout their lives.

## KŪLIA I KA NU'U

Ask your clients for referrals and get comfortable doing it. Don't be shy about this. Consider what you offer people—an opportunity to discover what's most important to them in life and the means to do what it takes to ensure they get what they need to have everything they desire. This is big. It's important. You have a lot to offer as a financial advisor. Never shy away from that truth.

Be that trusted, values-based advisor. And remember that trust is earned. It's also fragile. Work toward building that trusting relationship with all your clients, new and old. Once you get there, honor that dynamic. It's what differentiates us as Aloha Advisors.

Never betray a person's trust. It's not good for your prospects, your clients, or you, and it makes the wealth management industry in general look bad. Everything you do ripples, and we need to work together to improve the way people view financial advisors and the overall profession.

# IT'S THE PEOPLE, NOT THE PRODUCTS

Earlier I told you about my internship at a large life insurance company in Los Angeles. I then returned to Hawaii and worked for two years as an assistant sales manager at my father's company. They were grooming me to be the company's third-generation leader. I was a rookie and the boss's son, so no one there wanted my help. I hadn't paid my dues like they had, and though I qualified as a top advisor by production, that didn't count for much among the other financial advisors. If I were them, I'd simply assume that my father was giving me leads to help me do well. Of course, that wasn't the case.

I talked to my dad about my situation with the other advisors. My main concern was being of value to the firm and to do that which I needed to earn their respect—and my stripes. Even though I'd been immersed in and around all aspects of the life insurance business for three years during my internship, I didn't feel qualified to be the assistant manager of anything. In spite of his disagreement, I resigned and focused my attention toward financial planning.

I began my financial planning career selling life insurance. At the time, I was convinced that my products were good enough for anyone. In Hawaii, we could only represent one life insurance company. If I wanted products from another insurance company, I was required to ask for permission. Then I'd get a single case contractual agreement and a sign-off by both my company's and the other company's management. It was a bit cumbersome and, fortunately, this rarely occurred. I was always happy to sell what the company I worked for offered.

My first prospects were a couple—a lady I knew from high school and her husband. They were both attorneys, and even better, they wanted life insurance coverage to address potential loss of income that one may face upon the passing of the other. For me, it was a significant case, and I stood to make more money than I would otherwise have made in six months from the salary I left behind. This was my *first week* selling life insurance for a living!

The couple kept talking about a specific package offered by another insurance company. I tried to convince them that the product they wanted was no better than what I could offer them from my company. They were persistent. They knew the financials, and they were already sold on this other product and company.

I did all the work for them and because I failed to work with the other company to get the product, a financial advisor at that other company made a *lot* of money. Everyone was happy except me.

This was another significant learning experience. Apparently, not everyone wanted what I had to offer. It was a startling revelation, and I didn't understand it at first. I could take it personally and pretend they just weren't as informed as I was, or I could figure out why they felt this way and change the way I was doing things. I had to start educating myself beyond the company I represented and find out what else was going on out there in the financial world. I felt fortunate. It was early in my career, and I was mesmerized with the unknown and energized by the possibilities that my chosen path and future promised.

## FINANCIAL ADVISING FROM THE INSIDE OUT

Eventually I left Hawaii and moved to establish a brokerage firm for my father and his company in California. Their idea was to broaden the company's reach along the West Coast of the United States. There I discovered lots of financial products. There were products that outperformed ones from the company I represented back in Hawaii. There were products that did things my company's products didn't as well. And that's all before considering the many strategies that involved structures that took advantage of our country's tax codes. It was a whole new world and the beginnings of my journey toward understanding and embracing comprehensive wealth management.

Beyond life insurance, there was health insurance, pensions, IRAs, qualified plans, annuities, and more. The variety was endless. There was even more by way of the investment world. Then I began to integrate legal structuring that purposefully led to greater tax efficiencies and even better results.

That was when I realized that the best product in the world for one person doesn't translate to the right product for *everybody*. As a financial advisor, beginning your journey to discover what your prospects need doesn't start with your product. Instead of trying to figure out where you can fit the financial instruments you represent into a person's situation, you're better served to figure out what they need first and then go out and find it. It may be your product, or it may be someone else's.

And again, to figure out what people need, it's best to begin with the end in mind and find out what they want, which brings us back to focusing on our prospective client: who this person is and what is most important to them.

Each person is in a particular place in their life. They'll wish for different things based on who they are, where they are, and where they want to go. It's up to you to put your products aside and make that your focus. Once you know that, you can begin to look at the many possible ways to get them what they desire faster, more efficiently, effectively, and so forth.

# Values Based Approach

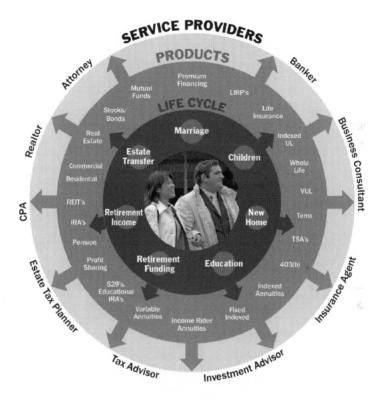

The values-based, "inside out" Aloha Advisor approach.

This is different from trying to shoehorn your product into a specific situation or need. It's an "inside out" approach, beginning with you and your prospects side by side on the inside, looking outward toward the future life they wish to shape and enjoy within the context of where they are in their lives and their financial reality, building a strategy and accessing best-suited products together, and then reaching out to engage other specialists and service providers to meet their hoped-for destinations. Compare that to the "outside in" traditional approach, where you're standing outside with your product trying to figure out how to squeeze it into your prospects' lives.

# Traditional Sales Approach

● Life Event
◀ Approach

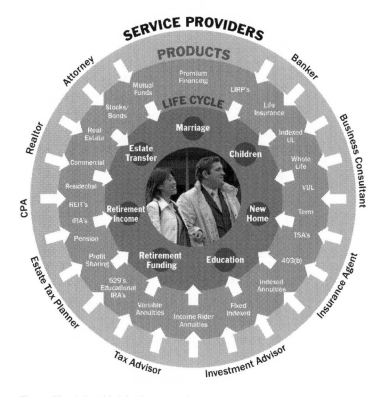

The traditional, "outside in" sales approach.

## THE PSYCHOLOGY OF PRODUCT-BASED SELLING

There are a lot of reasons not to sell products from the outside in. In the first place, you're automatically eliminating all the other potentially suitable products that may prove a better fit. Then you need to figure out how to get people to buy those other, less-effective items you represent and justify them into their lives. When it's not the best fit, how do you operate with a clear conscience?

Another issue I have with product-based selling is that so often it's presented as a solution. Solutions imply that there are problems to fix. When people tell me about themselves and what's important to them, they're not talking about problems. They tell me what they care about and what they want for these things, organizations, or people they care so much about whom they depend on or who depend upon them. Their wishes can usually be met by changing paths, a slight adjustment to their portfolio, or redirecting income toward different financial vehicles. They're looking to me to help them to adequately address certain needs, though we're certainly not referring to the most basic of needs like food, water, and shelter. They don't come to me because their basic needs aren't being met—they want fulfillment in their lives. They need to leverage their assets and cash flow to make that happen.

I'm not one for telling people that I have or am the solution to anything. I'm not a fan of making people think they have problems. It's a scare tactic that often works, and it's not at all what I do.

## KŪLIA I KA NU'U

You probably know all the details of your company and your

products inside and out, and that's great. You should be well versed in these things. That's a given. Just don't think they're the most important thing for you to know. For an advisor, selling products isn't the *most* important thing you do.

Your main job is getting to know your prospects and to understand and appreciate them for who they are and what they find of importance and to make sure that they know that you do. When they speak to you, listen. If they mention something that they want to happen in their lives, listen to the details of all that they want to transpire. Ask them more questions about it. Don't immediately allow your mind to jump to whatever product you might offer in your portfolio to fill their immediately found or proclaimed need. Imagine for a moment that there's more to the story and you're eager to understand all of it. Then imagine the many types of products and services to choose from, and from among those types, even more specific products and services. With all that variety, you stand equipped and at the ready to evolve from a product person into a people person focused on all that's important to others.

Try it. See how your prospects respond. I believe you'll be pleased with the outcome.

# WHAT YOUR CLIENTS SHOULD EXPECT FROM YOU

My focus wasn't *always* on my prospects and clients or on teaching other advisors to focus on theirs. I started my financial career with good intentions and was immediately taught to sell products. All the while, I firmly believed I was doing what I believed to be "my best" for those I helped secure products for along the way.

I learned about other products from other sectors of the financial world and the different issues they addressed, and that began to change my view of financial products in general and financial advising altogether. Something else happened that made me think differently. It had a profound effect on how I felt about people in this business who are engaged in our industry for the wrong reasons. Over the years, I watched other advisors intentionally take advantage of people—specifically, *my clients*—for their own benefit.

Though I am a holistic financial advisor, I'm generally known for my expertise in maximizing the value of life insurance related structures from varied country domiciles for their placement within wealthy global citizens' wealth transfer plans. It was in this role that I was called upon to receive a new prospect, an Asian businesswoman. She owned a hotel with a very successful restaurant in Japan and wanted to open a place in Hawaii. Her tax advisor needed someone to complete the life insurance portion of his fulfillment for this client. Cross-border planning between Japan and the US was a key area of specialization for me, so he saw me as a good fit and referred me in. I did not act as her lead financial advisor in any way and simply provided the life insurance benefit that promised her heirs the liquidity needed to pay the inheritance taxes that would become due upon her passing.

During this process, I received a host of frantic messages from her tax advisor. He discovered that our client's chosen lead financial advisor in Hawaii held a power of attorney over all her financial matters and accounts—even her bank accounts. The client's tax advisor and legal team were relying on and trusting this man without knowing he had been granted this power of attorney, and, worse, now they thought something was up. The client's finances were dwindling, and her plans were failing. They suspected the advisor entrusted with her finances didn't know what he was doing at the very *least* and was perhaps working purposefully to steal from her at the very *worst*. Since I was part of their extended plan for the client and I was local, they reached out to me to help find out if this was the case.

I met with the financial advisor and found out he wasn't licensed or trained to do much of *anything*. He couldn't answer my most basic questions. Yet armed with the title of "business consultant," he somehow convinced this woman to grant him access to all matters, including her money in the United States. This didn't make sense to me, because even if he was qualified to act on behalf of the client, he could have (and likely would have if his intentions were honest) asked for a *limited* power of attorney at best, granting him specific rights to do only what was necessary to fulfill his client's wishes.

Even though I didn't know the "victim" well, it infuriated me to see her being taken advantage of in this way. It was even worse that all involved parties were honoring his power of attorney and doing so without question. My team and I took on the painstaking effort to undo the damage done. It was a monumental task.

On another occasion, while away from my office I received a request from a Japanese businessman. He was thinking about buying or building a house in Hawaii and wanted to look at some property with me. Since he was arriving the next day, a Saturday, and I was still in New Jersey, I reached out to a member of my staff, who introduced him to a local realtor.

This realtor was well known in the islands for her success. From a casual glance, she was a perfect fit. She was fluent in Japanese, and most of her employees had been born and raised in Japan and spoke the language. I knew the realtor also had a reputation for being focused mainly on her own personal financial success, and that had me worried. I finished up my business in New Jersey, hopped on a plane back to Hawaii as quickly as I could, and was in the office by Tuesday. By then, my client—assisted by this realtor—had visited several properties on Saturday, presented offers on two of them on

Sunday, and then expedited escrow on Monday and immediately closed on both properties "as is" and in cash.

I got there one day, two properties, and tens of millions of dollars too late.

What the businessman didn't know was that the properties were priced more than 20 percent above market. Sure, the market itself was heated. Everything was selling at or just above market price at the time. Still, accepting an offer that high did not pass any proper realtor's due diligence, especially on properties of that asking price. Worse, there were no formal inspections conducted on the properties, and no lawyer was consulted to review the contracts, deeds, or any other legal papers. No one was asked to look at the details of the deal to see if it aligned with my client's financial plans. The whole transaction was out of compliance, and there was no accountability whatsoever to ensure proper handling of the sale. You might imagine egregious errors like this popping up occasionally in a modest and routine real estate deal. You might even expect to find some that cost a buyer a lot of money and heartache. This wasn't modest or routine. This was a jumbo multimillion-dollar purchase. *How does something like this happen?*

People who make huge purchases like this are best served by working with people they know and trust. Unfortunately, that's not always the case. When people want to buy something and there's no one like that available, they often go with the professional who's convenient and accessible. It may be someone they were referred to who speaks their language, shares their culture, or knows someone they know. In these cases, one client wanted to build a restaurant and the other client wanted a second home to go along with a rental home in paradise. They wanted to buy property and needed someone to help them. Ultimately, they entrusted their money with people who either weren't qualified to rightfully deliver what they wanted or didn't care enough about them to place their best interests ahead of their own. In one case, the "advisor" was both unqualified and malicious.

People expect advisors in *any* profession to act in their clients' best interests, and they have a right to expect that. *It's what people should expect from advisors like me and you.* In the case of seeking an ideal realtor, these people came to someone they trusted—me. They ended up with another kind of advisor, and because I wasn't there to look out for them, they were taken for a multimillion-dollar ride. Incidentally, twelve years after buying those properties for 20 percent above market, the client sold one of them—for a little more than the price they originally paid. I'm grateful that they thoroughly enjoyed the properties and even more grateful that, in the end, the amount they invested found its way back to them.

## OVERCOMING BIASES

The side effect of deals like these are clients who lose trust in anyone with whom they do business. People can be naturally cynical and mistrusting, especially when they meet with a professional for the first time who has something to gain from the relationship. A bad experience only serves to reinforce that cynicism. No matter how genuine you are, they may be waiting for the "gotcha" moment when you show your true salesperson colors and ask for the sale. It's on you to help them overcome that natural bias.

My best advice to you is *patience*. You'll often contend with this bias, but people will eventually learn that you are who you say you are, not a phony. Keep an open heart and a quiet mind instead of automatically dipping into your portfolio of products. Focus on the person in front of you, and you'll see what I mean.

Your clients expect you to earn their trust and prove their bias wrong. This is tough for some advisors to stomach, but the best of the best let this bias roll off of them. Those who take it personally lose. They let it get to them, and that bias inspires hate. You must be careful what you hate, or you could become it. You could become that advisor whom biased prospects see you as, and that isn't good for you or for them. The way I learned to deal with this bias was by simply allowing people their opinion, again, without judgment. My job is to simply understand and appreciate where they're coming from. I don't have to agree with it, and I certainly don't own it—it's theirs. Leave it at that.

## IT'S NOT ABOUT WHAT YOU HAVE

Your prospects and clients should also expect you to understand that they do not necessarily care about your products. The businessman and businesswoman who were taken advantage of didn't want to know about all the properties available or about the properties that would earn the realtor or the financial advisor the biggest commission. These clients were only interested in real estate that met their wants and needs.

People generally don't care about all your products or the products from other financial advisors for that matter. They don't spend a lot of time thinking about insurance, investments, banking, taxes, or the law. The exception is the occasional, potential customer (versus prospect and eventual client) who's already made up their mind about a specific product they want to buy.

In fact, prospects may *fear* your products—and fear that you may influence them to buy a product that doesn't satisfy their wants.

People do, however, care about what your products can do for them. This is hard to wrap your head around when product sales are the main focus of your company. It's what you spend a lot of your time learning—what you have and how to sell it instead of the hopes and concerns those products address.

When we ask people the right questions, begin to uncover what they care about, and do this well, people stop thinking about what we sell. They begin to think about those things they care about. They think about their families. They think about the home they want to raise their children in and the schools they want to send them to. They think about the car they want to drive, the vacations they want to take, and how they're going to spend their retirement years.

That's what's important in their lives. Your products and services, if anything, are simply a burden to them: something they must figure out that will cost them money. If you're focused on your product and selling it, think about the message you're sending to this person. They want you to see them and understand what they care about. They expect you to understand why they came to see you in the first place. They care about something so much that they pushed past the concept that your product is a burden and made a point of coming to see you, because they know that somehow what you offer is what they need in order to get what they desire. You need to understand that and respect it by putting them and what they seek first.

If you do this and provide a meaningful plan for them, you'll release their burdens. It will be liberating. When they get a reminder to deposit their quarterly savings, a bill in the mail for that disability insurance policy or something else in their plan, they stop seeing it as a bill. It's an investment in themselves. It's what they're doing to keep their life on track. This only happens when you have those conversations, recognize what's important to people, confirm that it is of importance to them, and steer them toward their hopeful future in a better way than they did before meeting you.

They aren't experts in finance. They're experts in their own lives, and they'll prove it to you if you ask them enough questions. You don't need to prove to them how much you know about your products to gain their trust. You do have to prove that you care enough about them to learn about them and what they want.

This doesn't require a lot of preparation. Like I mentioned earlier in this book, I come to my first prospect meeting with a notebook, a pen, an open heart, and a quiet mind. My most important preparation is to be quiet and listen. I bring my core values, and I give gratitude—Mahalo—that I get to listen and learn about this person's life. I mean that. Think about what's most precious in life. It's other people. How blessed am I to have the opportunity to really get to know another human being who values life and those who enjoy it with them?

## TRUST BY ASSOCIATION

At the beginning of this chapter, I told you a couple of stories about people—my clients—who I believe weren't honestly served. I took these incidents personally because they affected people who placed their trust in me. In fact, there's no doubt that my clients trusted these other advisors *because* they trusted me. They believed that since I acted in their best interests, anyone with whom I associated would certainly do the same. Unfortunately, that failed to be the case. The realtor unconscionably made more than a million bucks off the relationship of trust I built with my client, and I never wanted to allow that to happen again.

These incidents inspired me to revisit my guiding principles, core values, and intended outcomes, and that led me to rethink the organizational structure of my company. I needed a system of checks and balances between the financial advisors I called upon to assist my clients. Advisors who might bring greater value to the relationship yet weren't *purposefully* connected had no accountability to me or to anyone. They could act in whatever manner they pleased. And while I, and *any* referring advisor, expect every professional brought in to do a good job, there are no assurances or guarantees that that will happen.

It was clearly time to start a collaborative. An advisor who takes advantage of clients referred to them from within their collaborative risks their reputation with the entire supporting team and all its prospective referring advisors. A larger and purposefully arranged collaborative offers the opportunity to filter through many advisors from different disciplines as well as from similar ones.

At the time, I had no formalized collaborative. Whenever a

prospect needed someone with more in-depth knowledge than I carried on a particular topic, I simply referred them to an advisor who specialized in that respective field. In hindsight, shame on me. I had no oversight and no accountability. That didn't work for my clients, and because it didn't work for them, there was no way it could possibly work for me.

I now ask myself, "Why did I allow these things to happen?" Truthfully, I think that, as financial advisors, we become numb to this behavior without realizing it. We desensitize. What do we know about those areas of financial specialization outside of our expertise? How can we be accountable and responsible for the actions of other professionals? And when these experts end up circumventing best practices, we tell ourselves that it's "just a salesperson doing their job." Until it happens to one of our clients. Or a member of our family. Or us.

By allowing myself to become numb to it, I felt like I was condoning it. *It's just business.* Was it? Is this how we should be treating one another, what we should expect from the people we do business with, and what we're willing to accept from those to whom we introduce people we care about?

None of this aligned with my core values. Going along with it wasn't who I was or how I wanted to live my life. Angry and ashamed, I had to do something about how I felt. The answer was to focus on the person, always—focus on the person in front of me. Be clear on what I do best and seek out worldwide experts in the areas of the financial world that I knew less about—banking, taxes, the law, and even in specialized parts of insurance and investments—to do those things they do best. Play the role of a truly committed lead advisor and carefully vet any other advisors I bring in to work with clients and figure out ways to hold them accountable. This had to happen if I was going to truly take care of my clients. I'd better choose well.

I was on the right path with my consultative approach and toward sharing more Aloha. Armed with the right intentions, I was serving people for the right reasons, and doing good to do better, just not yet to the best of my abilities. I was allowing other advisors to mistreat people who relied on me for guidance and care. This affected my ability to do my job—to help my clients fulfill their lives—and it affected me personally because it was not aligned with my core values. People expected me to be trustworthy, and they expected anyone I associated with to be trustworthy, too. They still do.

## KŪLIA I KA NU'U

You may be currently associating with other advisors. Do you trust them? Ask yourself if you'd refer a good friend or family member to them. Would you trust them with *your* finances if you needed expertise from their area of specialization? If your answer is "no," please stop sending your precious clients to them.

You hold high standards for yourself, and it's critical to maintain those same standards for the people to whom you refer others. It takes great effort to find those advisors you need to broaden and deepen your capabilities and who also meet your high standards. Still, it's what you and your clients deserve.

If you encounter a prospect with biases against you, your industry, or financial advisors in general, don't take it personally. Let them have that opinion. It's theirs to keep—for now. Take it upon yourself to prove them wrong by being the best advisor possible.

# WORKING WITHIN A COLLABORATIVE TO DELIVER FOR YOUR CLIENTS

Several events put me on a path toward starting a collaborative. I didn't like seeing my clients being taken advantage of by other advisors. I didn't like the fact that some of my prospects and clients were using numerous tax advisors and segregating their assets between them so no one advisor saw the whole picture. Frankly, I didn't like a lot of things.

There's a card trick where you have a person pick a card, face-down, from a deck and without looking at it, hand it to you. Then, *you* sneak a look at it, hide it in your pocket, and ask them a series of questions to identify the card. You start by asking them to pick clubs and spades or hearts and diamonds. If the card is a club (or a spade) and they choose clubs and spades, then you say, "Great, so the card is a club or a spade."

But if the card is a heart or a diamond and they choose clubs and spades, you say, "Great, that leaves hearts and diamonds." Then you ask them to choose between twos through tens or jacks, queens, kings, and aces. Again, depending on the card and their choice, you narrow down the selection either to what they choose *or* to whatever they *do not* choose. You keep narrowing the range of possibilities until the person miraculously "chooses" the hidden card, which you dramatically pull from your pocket and reveal to the audience. Ooh, ahh. You're basically manipulating the person into selecting the card that's in your pocket—the only card you have. You'd be amazed how easy it is to fool people with this simple trick.

This is what it's like to have one thing to sell. You make people believe they're *choosing* that product when in reality, you're manipulating them into asking you for the one thing you have. The only card in your pocket. Some people are very good at this. At first glance, you might think they're great negotiators. Too often what they're really good at is manipulating people into wanting the only product they have to sell.

Working on your own, without a collaborative, is like that. You can do everything I talk about in this book, even ask all the right questions; ultimately, you must figure out what your clients need to satisfy their desires. If you don't have that thing, you're going to be tempted to manipulate them into believing they need the one thing that you've got. You see the end in sight, the outcome. You have one card in your pocket, and the endgame is already decided.

To do the most good for people, I need to see all their wants so I can offer them the best options available. This means uncovering all their wishes as they relate to what they're saving, preserving, or planning to give away and figuring out where I and whatever products and services I might represent—the cards of the deck of financial opportunities I hold—fit. It also means seeing where it makes sense to bring in other advisors with specialized knowledge and sometimes even products, too—the cards I do not have in that deck of opportunities. I need those specialists working with me prepared to work with my clients, and I need to trust them to deliver on the promises they make.

## LIMITLESS FINANCIAL ADVISING

Working within a collaborative, you're no longer limited to providing your clients with only your products and services, so while your consultative process may not change, the outcomes you provide become more encompassing. You're equipped to offer people more ways to satisfy their wants.

Once you begin consulting in this way, you quickly realize that the value of your competencies is maximized. You truly trust the other advisors and feel comfortable and secure turning to them to assist with any plan fulfillment. You can consult with these specialists with complete confidence, knowing that whatever your clients need to make what they want to happen will happen. You can deliver whatever they need personally or together with your alliances. As their lead advisor, you can take a holistic approach to the consulting process and deliver better outcomes for them.

To get there, you must understand the specialists within your collaborative and the various opportunities they represent. This is not to say that you have to know the details of every product and service of every company you collaborate with;

you must, however, have a basic understanding of what they do and how they do it, and you *must* know that you can trust them, not only to deliver what your clients need delivered but to treat them the way you want them treated. Or, going back to the Platinum Rule, the way *your clients* want to be treated!

From there, you'll be prepared to ask your questions freely and discover what's important to your prospects, knowing that you can help them and convert them to loyal clients and advocates. You *know* you can—and teams of professionals stand behind you whom you can call upon whenever you need them. This leaves you open to focus completely on the person in front of you without worrying about if or how you're going to meet all their hopes and concerns. You know this person will more than likely become a client who is comfortable relying on you for all matters and eventually promote you as your advocate.

Suddenly, products are no longer a barrier to your prospect's success. You can ask them all those questions you may have either been afraid to ask or steered away from in the past. You can find out what they're *not* achieving right now that they'd like to achieve, and what they *are* achieving that they'd like to do better. You can ask them what's important to them about... *anything*.

## A GOOD COLLABORATIVE IS PURPOSEFUL

A collaborative can be formal or informal. You might join an existing one, start your own, or simply reach out to specialists who complement what you do and offer what you need to help your clients better than you could without them.

In the financial planning world, people need advisors in banking, insurance, investments, tax, and the law. Within each category, there are many areas of specialization. From one place to another, country to country, the expertise narrows and diverges even further. Each person's life is unique, and so their wants and needs are also going to be unique. When you're vetting expertise for your collaborative, consider the "gaps" in financial planning that you can't fill on your own and seek professionals whose areas of specialization fill them. Look for companies that specialize, too, because the more expertise you align at the ready, the better prepared you are to deliver plans of action to help a broader and more diverse group of individuals and companies. You'll become a most treasured advisor.

As lead advisor, think of yourself as the architect of your client's financial planning home. Through your consulting process, you help them draw a plan of what they'd want their house to look like. Depending on what their house looks like right now, they may need major renovations, or you might have to design a whole new house for them. Remember, you're the lead advisor—the *architect*, not the *plumber*. You'll need to bring in the best people to help build that dream home— carpenters, electricians, painters, and roofers. Your prospect may need an interior decorator and a landscaper, and you facilitate that, too. The lead advisor who works with a collaborative doesn't simply refer people to other specialists for, say, banking assistance. Like an architect working with other specialists to create someone's dream home, the work is organized, aligned, and complementary. That's one of its greatest strengths. You and the companies within your supporting team aren't working against each other or competing for budgets, because you're all building the same house, with you as the architect.

## OHANANET

My company, The Pacific Bridge Companies (TPBC), is composed of a significant group of corporations and the like that I built to collaborate with various financial disciplines from around the globe. As the world continues to internationalize nation by nation, we seek to bring global financial navigation to life. This means bringing down the walls between nations: the walls represented by regulations, products, legal access, taxation, language, culture, currency, and other differences that challenge us as people and companies, especially when venturing into and out of countries outside of our homes. Together, these subsidiaries and affiliates of TPBC aim to provide comprehensive global wealth management services.

As an advisor, there are rules and regulations that I must abide by within my country. This is much the same across the many disciplines in the world of financial planning, and I must account for my duties, obligations, and responsibilities in whatever business and country that we choose to involve ourselves. It can become quite convoluted when putting together a wealth management plan across many disciplines spread across different countries. Having these corporations as separate entities allows us to legally operate within this global landscape and provide increasingly greater value as we do so.

The Pacific Bridge Companies vets financial professionals from within a larger collaborative called OhanaNet that includes banking, insurance, investment, tax, and legal professionals from around the world who share the simple belief that together, we're better as advisors and better for the people who depend on our advice and counsel. We're launching our global financial navigation efforts primarily through the individual advisors of OhanaNet. Large financial institutions currently have little incentive to drive this forward. They face much risk in promoting a structure such as this before the world screams for it, especially given all the associated challenges, industry protection regulations, and differing consequences due to legal access and assessed taxation. Because of this, I believe that individual advisors, helping their global citizens navigate, must press global financial navigation forward through collaborative initiatives.

A collaborative such as OhanaNet, though still in its infantile state, is a purposeful mission of worth. It's currently my larger-than-life effort. We've created a process of purposeful engagement from within this greater collaborative that is more than simply a group of advisors ready and willing to support one another. Advisors who convert from OhanaNet members to TPBC's Ohana *Firms* leverage their competencies to ensure a broad and deep level of expertise that can fully accommodate clients navigating between Asia and the United States, if not around the globe.

Each of us represents certain areas of specialization, and those who agree to engage stand prepared to share resources when called upon by another member. While we may sometimes share the same area of specialization, each of us delivers our expertise in unique ways, and because of this, our value propositions differ. Regardless, we help each other create and execute plans, all the while learning and growing stronger and faster by working together. This in turn allows us to do better for our clients.

And just as we do with clients, working with each other in our collaborative begins with discovery. We ask questions and find out what's important to the firms we work with and the people they serve. We learn *how* they serve people, *how* they work with their vendors, and *how* they interact with each other. We engage with them in a way they want to engage, and because of this, we get the most from the relationship. Ohana Firms are, simply put, Ohana—*family*.

Financial advisors who join OhanaNet can create their own select group of complementary businesses, just as we have, or they can consider becoming an Ohana Firm of TPBC, if they're a good fit. Then, instead of thinking about how they're going to sell their products, they can think about how they're going to serve people.

Sometimes you need to look outside yourself and to another specialist for the answer. With your collaborative team in place, you can confidently do so. This isn't scary. It's powerful. It's freeing. Focusing on clients and knowing you have many experts to rely on is the ideal place to be for a financial advisor. You don't have to worry about how well your products serve people on all matters. You don't have to worry that you're not a real estate expert or a tax expert. In a proper collaborative, there's always an appropriate professional available who you can count on to help your clients.

This goes both ways, because while I enjoy the freedom of having trusted professionals to call on whenever I need them, they know they can call on me as well—and they do. Working this way reminds me of my grandfather L. T. and what he worked to accomplish: delivering access and opportunity to anyone who could benefit, regardless of their race or country of origin. With my companies, I legally provide access to total wealth management services and products to people around the world without boundaries. In Asia, we're providing access to products and services from outside of their countries such as the United States. We also assist first-generation ethnic communities from Asia in the US with their wealth management concerns across many disciplines as they migrate to and from the United States.

I created this collaborative to enable global financial navigation. I come from a country, the United States, that's populated by people from many countries. Due to the ease of global travel, we can visit other places, fall in love with other cities, and enjoy spending time in countries worldwide. We're unencumbered geographically, yet we're restricted when it comes to finances. This is the importance of global financial navigation to me—it reduces or removes those boundaries.

## COLLABORATIVES VS. CONTRACTUAL RELATIONSHIPS

Some companies don't rely on formal collaboratives. Instead, they might reach out directly to other companies for services they don't otherwise provide through *contractual relationships*. Banks that offer complementary financial products from investment and insurance organizations are fine examples. The bank provides contracted access to solicit these products with the intent to augment whatever core products and services the bank offers directly. The bank's core offerings may lean toward items such as loans and deposits, and not toward other ways of providing income or accumulating wealth. Clients may see the bank as less than adequate without these other financial products. At the same time, banks must meet their financial goals and targets just like any other for-profit business. Providing access to these added opportunities is one way to help keep customers happy and ensure funds remain within the bank's control, all the while creating new and additional sources of income to the bank.

Like most financial institutions, banks want their customers to remain with them and expand their assets with them. At the same time, they don't want to cannibalize their portfolios by placing monies into long-term investments outside of their direct offerings. So they especially like complementary services that necessitate the involvement of their core bank products. While this isn't necessarily regrettable for the investor, it's not always ideal, either.

I witnessed this firsthand visiting with a certain financial service organization that was tied to a bank. Their conversations seemed to continuously revolve around how these services and the combination of such might best encourage higher returns on shareholder equity. While they spoke of the potential of new services, they were primarily focused on profitability to the shareholders of the company.

The dynamic is much different between companies in a collaborative that purposefully aligns its members to effectively engage with one another. Each company works toward the same goal of developing the best plan for the client. There's little room for ulterior motives, especially when these companies establish and maintain relationships built on trust. Each professional is required to show each individual, whether it's their client or a person who was referred to them from another advisor, the same respect. They all are expected to dedicate themselves toward delivering the best outcome for that person, albeit from their respective involved area of expertise.

Going back to the example of building a financial house

for your client: though members of a collaborative may be like-minded in the sense that they're committed to working together for the good of the client, each comes with their own unique expertise, talent, and personality. It's up to you, the lead advisor (the architect), to ensure that whatever these members bring to the table fits the client and the team and stands in agreement and in line with the overall plan.

Say you hire a top contractor—the best in the business. That contractor, without consulting anyone else on the project, installs gold fixtures throughout the house. The fixtures may look wonderful—do they go with the rest of the house? Do they complement the home's architecture, style, or color palette? Will they leave you with enough money to hire a painter or an electrician? A good architect doesn't allow those they call on to go astray from delivering to their plan. They're going to call on a contractor they know and trust to install fixtures that match the whole house and fit the budget.

## BEST PRACTICES IN THE UNITED STATES

In the US, many financial planners create collaboratives with the intent to provide their financial services more holistically. Firms might involve insurance and investment advisors who coordinate their different areas of expertise such as income replacement, retirement, education planning, general wealth building, business planning, and estate planning. Each of these specialists may also arrange their own circle of advisors who complement their chosen discipline.

This team concept is good and considered a best practice. I prefer to extend my circle beyond simply providing access to expertise within limited areas of specialization. While I also have advisors like these who complement what I do, I also enlist the services of bankers, insurance and investment specialists, tax advisors, and attorneys from a variety of categories representing specific and, at times, unique products, services, and areas of expertise from around the world.

Limiting yourself to one advisor for any one field is like going to your primary care doctor for a heart murmur or a broken leg. You might start with your doctor. You'll be glad that there are cardiologists and orthopedic surgeons in your physician's network. You'll be even happier if your doctor knows the specialists they refer you to and makes their best efforts to find those who best fit for the outcome you seek.

### WHY CAN'T I DO THIS ON MY OWN?

It's OK to want to do everything on your own. The question is should you? Are you equipped to, and if not, should you learn what's necessary to be an expert in all the fields your clients need an expert in? If you choose to go this route, to whom do you refer clients who require other experts in the meantime?

Many advisors choose to go at it alone. They may not want to join a collaborative because they're afraid of losing business to another advisor. They worry that if they introduce a client to another advisor, they'll lose control of the account and possibly lose the client. This fear isn't without warrant because other advisors *can* (and some actually will) take people away from you. If you think your advisor-client relationship isn't strong enough for them to want to stay with you, you have a valid concern.

Another reason some advisors choose to go at it alone is

because they're embarrassed to reach out to others for their expertise. They fear the thought of their clients thinking that they're ignorant and that there's something they don't know enough about that may better fit their financial plan. Worse, some advisors are embarrassed to approach other advisors, simply because they don't want them thinking they're lacking certain expertise. Our egos are strong. They get in the way.

It comes down to insecurity. This fear of being "not good enough" is real. However, if you're successful in this business, you are very good at something, and probably a specialist in your area. It's great if you're a specialist. The world needs specialists, and if you're especially interested in a certain aspect of wealth management, please pursue it. Just don't let that get in the way of calling on other experts when your clients' wants and needs demand it.

There are advisors who work with other advisors yet not in a truly coordinated way. They might be in a "producer group," which are advisors in similar fields, such as investments and insurance, who work together. There are networks and organizations, too. Whatever the case, a purposeful collaborative is preferred. There is proactive and ongoing learning between advisors. There is alignment in what we do and how we work with our clients. We share information openly, with the goal of serving people to the best of our combined ability.

## PROTECTING YOURSELF IN A COLLABORATIVE

Collaborative relationships aren't always successful. They depend on the trustworthiness, skills, expertise, products, services, and intentions of the people in them. You may trust your clients to another advisor, but sometimes the chemistry simply isn't right. Other times, they may fail your clients, in which case they fail you as well. Do whatever you can to prevent that from happening, and if it does, be prepared to confront the advisor to let them know you're taking your clients to someone else and why.

While there is a certain amount of accountability within an alliance, it's difficult to manage the behaviors of other professionals. For this reason, you may want to personally vet professionals from each field and maintain an inner circle within the collaborative: a group of professionals with whom you maintain close relationships, who know what you do and how you do it, and who are as committed to the same level of Pono as you are to serve clients and to do so together with you, much like my company's Ohana Firms.

Identify people you trust in banking, insurance, investment, tax, and law. Look for people you'd call on for guidance with your own finances. Nurture relationships with these people and find out how broad and how deep they are within their areas of expertise. Find out what they do, how they do it, and why they do it. This isn't a cursory checklist—take some time and formalize this process. You need to believe with certainty that you can and should introduce your best clients to these people without reservation or concern. They should feel the same about you.

In a collaborative of 5,000 members, you may have forty professionals in your inner circle. You may have five. These are the professionals you work with on a regular basis. As you identify the need to add areas of expertise, you can recruit new members to join your circle.

Ensure you're bringing value to each member. Establish

educational platforms for these collaborators. Identify areas where you can share resources. Set up regular face-to-face meetings so you can stay connected and committed to the same cause: your clients.

If you don't make this effort, you may end up with a group of disconnected people who aren't bringing any value to each other or to the group. That's not a collaborative.

Think about the social networking groups you belong to. Take LinkedIn, for example. It's a terrific platform if you actively use it, and when you don't, those connections with other people become rather meaningless. They serve no purpose and have no value.

Pay attention to who's truly engaged in your professional circle. Some advisors will recognize the benefit immediately and want to participate or contribute, while others will not be so eager to get involved. Your collaborative may shift and change over time as you engage, re-engage, and disengage from one another.

Once your alliances are formally in place, the benefits become obvious. Your increased access to deeper levels of expertise across myriad professions, represented by many more professionals, makes yours a more valued practice. These people have access to you, too, and they'll have the opportunity to refer you to those who need your services. When everyone is providing their best guidance, you win, the other advisors win, and your clients win.

Finally, as you engage other professionals, always keep in mind that it's up to you to maintain your relationship with your clients, to remain committed to them, and to do so as their lead financial advisor. While you appreciate those of other disciplines, everything starts and ends with you. The financial strategies deployed must complement each other and satisfy the goals identified in your consultative discovery discussions.

## KŪLIA I KA NU'U

Think about the areas of expertise in which you excel within your financial advisory, and then think about the areas where you don't have that same level of expertise. Are there services or products you provide that aren't always the best for your clients due to a lack of meaningful options? Are there services or products that you currently don't provide that may prove of value to your clients?

Where *else* are your clients going for wealth management expertise and guidance? If you're unable to provide them with the best professionals, products, and services for banking, insurance, investment, tax, and law, who do you know in these fields that is on par in their attention, care, and expertise with what you do and how you do it?

Start with a self-discovery and see where you could do better for your clients. Don't be in a hurry to put together a broad and massive number of professionals. Choose people carefully and start your own collaborative.

I warn you against relying on others to do this for you. Find your own why. Think about why you want to do this, just as I did. Then go out and find your own team. You're the one who will be working with them. You're going to be introducing your clients to these people. Choose your own Ohana.

You can also join an existing alliance to access, sift, and funnel through. You're welcome to join mine. See where you can benefit from working with others, and then find the people in OhanaNet that fit you—what you do and how you do it.

OhanaNet includes professionals from around the world who share the simple belief that together, we're better for the people who depend on our advice and counsel.

From there, develop your own circle of professionals to collaborate with. I take great care in selecting these people. For example, I might have 300 tax advisors in Korea to work with, yet I may only sincerely know about twenty of them. From those twenty, it's up to me to decide which ones are the best fit for my clients and me. A collaborative may have hundreds of tax advisors. That doesn't mean you collaborate with all of them or that they'll do the same with you.

From among these twenty tax advisors, for example, I must learn what they do, how they do it, and why they do it. I want to make sure that our philosophes align. I may lean toward working with a tax advisor who already shares a client with me. I'll also test their expertise and consider their reputation and other ways they contribute to their clients and the industry.

Whether you start your own collaborative or join one, these are the steps you'll want to take to build your circle of professionals.

# WHAT YOUR CLIENTS NEED TO KNOW ABOUT WORKING WITH A COLLABORATIVE

A financial institution in Japan was reviewing a very large life insurance policy recommended to their client's company in the US to help support the funding of a retirement payout and stock buyout in another country. Given the fact that the structure, product, and ownership were to originate through a company operating in the United States, the firm sought assistance from me. Coincidentally, they were vetting my firm on related matters at the same time. They spent two weeks in California and Hawaii getting to know us.

I was asked if I'd be willing to fly from LA to Japan for a one-hour visit with their client before flying home. The reason for this request was simply to address their general concerns about the overall plan and its potential results. I readily agreed and contacted a noteworthy international tax firm that I had been collaborating with and asked them to join the meeting as well.

In our review, we discovered that the structure of the plan and the products it delivered wouldn't meet their client's objectives. The plans looked great on paper—very sexy, numbers-wise. Our SWOT analysis indicated that it couldn't do what was being promised. Incidentally, everyone in the meeting spoke Japanese except for me, so I had my most trusted interpreter travel with me. Needless to say, it was an expensive meeting for me. After I presented my analysis, the tax advisor made a few supporting comments, and we left.

It was an inappropriate plan for the firm's client, and to make matters worse, the policies placed as recommended would have been subjected to certain double taxation. Furthermore, their proposals as presented violated federal laws. Fortunately, I made the decision to get on that plane with my colleague and brought in the international tax firm to ensure proper tax-related assessments.

I wasn't paid to fly to Japan or spend my time in that meeting. I went to help the firm that knew they didn't have the expertise to provide proper counsel on a significant transaction to their client. Because I formally agreed to collaborate with them and to work in true partnership on matters of potential concern that may involve my expertise, I was there to ensure that they were doing things right.

When I returned to my office in the states, a fax message awaited me. (By the way, a *fax* is a machine we used to regularly transmit messages and documents in the Dark Ages.) It was from the financial institution. Their client wanted to hire me. What an incredibly welcome surprise!

The outcome of the meeting was that I was hired, my international tax firm collaborator's comments were corroborated by theirs, and I was ultimately able to pay them for their involvement. We proved to this individual and the firm that we were committed to doing things right and not just to making a sale. That choice—getting on that plane—kept the client's name out of the papers and kept the financial institution out of trouble, too. And we ultimately earned a lot of money. So there was that unplanned side benefit as well. My interpreter? She now runs one of our key companies and is an officer of our holding company.

For clients, it always pays to work with an advisor who's part of an effective collaborative.

### LOYALTY TO YOUR LEAD FINANCIAL ADVISOR

The financial institution shared their Aloha with me because of their Aloha for their client. I was filled with Mahalo, grateful they had brought me in. They had good intentions yet were short on expertise in certain areas, and bringing my firm in as a collaborator was a smart thing to do. They did this because of Pono, as they insist upon doing the right things right for their clients. I didn't know where the opportunity would lead. I simply knew that they needed help and that my expertise was being called on. They trusted me, so I trusted them. It's what you do for Ohana.

People involved in similar situations should stick by their advisor and avoid attempting to replace them with other firms from within the supporting team, especially when their advisor was the one who introduced them to these valued professionals. Collaborators brought in by other advisors should never steal their clients away, either, regardless of the promise that new relationship may represent.

Not all firms handle people in the same way, and each relationship is unique. To your clients, working with several firms can feel disjointed and uncoordinated at times. This is another reason they should always look to you as their lead financial advisor and that trusting relationship for guidance as they receive help from others. The lead advisor carries the big picture of what they want and will ultimately be the one who's looking out for them. As questions and confusion arise, you're the one person your client should be calling on to ensure that all aligns with their intentions.

Another issue that occasionally raises its head may involve the relationship between your client and your referred advisor. They may not hit it off. Make sure your client knows that they never have to work with professionals you refer them to that fail to earn or keep their confidence. They should know that they can always rely on you to manage these relationships on their behalf, as you're the one responsible for introducing them to these experts in order to fulfill your promises to them as their lead financial advisor. They should always let you know what's working and what isn't for them.

This happened to me, and the situation kind of took me by surprise. I had a long-tenured client who was an engineer. I introduced him to a chartered financial analyst whom I often called upon to help me with certain investment advisory relationships. Two analytical types—they'd surely hit it off.

They didn't. I love this investment guru. My client didn't like him at all. The investment advisor wasn't doing anything wrong, yet this person disliked him so much that he refused to follow any of his advice. In my coordinated efforts, each professional I call on for help remains closely aligned, and our supporting process ensures our constant involvement. So my client simply communicated his displeasure, and I called on another who's proven a better fit for his personality.

Despite these occasional challenges, collaboratives usually provide a better measure of accountability and service than you'll find with traditional contractual relationships. As the lead financial advisor, take responsibility for your clients' relationships with other professionals in the supporting team. Your clients should know that you are very much involved no matter who you send them to and that you're there to handle anything that may arise.

As I look back on introductions that led to less-than-ideal outcomes for my clients, I realize that some of these issues could have been prevented had I made it clear to these clients to call me as questions or concerns arose about advisors I sent them to and always when advisors made recommendations to them before taking any steps forward. If the businessman who made that huge real estate investment had just picked up the phone and said, "Stephen, here's what I'm going to do, but I'm not really sure about it," I wouldn't have necessarily stopped the deal; I certainly would have advised him to demand proper due diligence and, at least in this case, wait for me to arrive to help him see it through. Of course, my mistake was in assuming that he'd call me before he acted in the first place. That's my bad.

## YOUR ADVISOR KNOWS WHAT THEY'RE BEST AT

Since that real estate debacle and the many situations that followed, we established a company dedicated to helping individuals and companies access real estate opportunities and expertise in much more formal terms. Our setup is unique, as we typically don't directly involve ourselves in the real estate transaction. Instead, we deliver real estate opportunities through best-in-class practitioners—brokers, operators, developers, and managers—from the varied products and locations from around the United States. If the deal is for residential property, we aim to matchmake with the top residential property brokers in the area. This is our intent anywhere, in any country. The real estate professional does their best in their area of specialization, and our firm coordinates the competencies and provides cultural and language expertise, along with an understanding and appreciation of all that's important to our clients. It's our responsibility to arrange for the appropriate cache of advisors to successfully execute on our clients' behalf through our collective experience, expertise, and resources.

While we understand real estate, we're not the best in the world at real estate in every sector of the business in every region, nor do we aspire to be so. My company knows its strengths, and we strive to be the best every day at those things. We know to deliver best in any sector demands that we either make the effort to be the best or seek partners who are among the best within their sector. Our goal is to always align ourselves with others of greatness, celebrate their unique talents, and engage with them for the benefit of those we serve.

No one advisor can know of all the rules and details in and around every specialty. Some are excellent and maintain extensive and expansive knowledge around many fields. Still, there are many opportunities, pitfalls, laws, strategies, products, philosophies, regulations, and so forth in every segment of wealth management. In some instances, we might have some expertise in the matter while other times—such as with legal advice—we trust the attorney to do what's right for the person. A specialist such as a tax attorney may not be able to figure out what someone really wants in their life, but they can help the person find certain outcomes within the attorney's area of specialization. This reality is further compounded when we venture outside of our local jurisdictions and cross state lines and country borders.

This is a critical benefit for anyone working with an advisor in a proper collaborative. The lead advisor's focus isn't on selling anything—it's on making sure that whatever they or their collaborating partners provide satisfies the individual. They do this by choosing the best people they can, based on what they know about these individuals, and by keeping the lines of communication open between themselves, the other advisors, and the client.

People should be able to trust their lead advisor to direct them to professionals they believe to be best-in-class for each of their specific needs. They need to also know that they can and should always rely upon their lead advisor for overarching guidance and advice. This is the person who earned their trust and will always put their interests first, ahead of anyone else, including other professionals in their supporting team. This is the person who did their best to understand what is of importance to them to live a happy and fulfilled life. This is the person who can ensure that the professionals involved are on target and on point for them as plans and goals evolve and as life happens.

## SHARING ALOHA IN A COLLABORATIVE

I can't speak for all financial advisors in every collaborative. As for me, I approach working with other advisors as an opportunity to meet more people and learn from them. I'm grateful for this, filled with Mahalo. Before I meet with other advisors whom I hope may believe it of value to work with me for the benefit of others, just as before I meet with my prospects, I remind myself to avoid being judgmental. I tell myself to toss my personal opinions to the side and trust in the fact that these relationships with specialists from across the financial planning spectrum allow me to deliver more and find better answers, rather than relying solely on my own experience and knowledge.

If an advisor believes in selling their product first and foremost and what people want comes second, I won't judge them. I won't go out of my way to engage with them, either. The same is true from within the collaborative. There are plenty of firms like that out there, so advisors and clients alike must remain vigilant. This isn't to say their represented products or services aren't worthy, and they may even prove best for the client in certain situations. Selling ahead of themselves still can prove a major problem. If an advisor begins their client-focused conversation talking about their product instead of confirming what they understand about the person's desires, that's a pretty good sign that they're more concerned with selling than with helping.

I want to work with other professionals who care about people and what's important to them. Clients should apply that same litmus test to any professional their lead advisor refers them to and hold us accountable.

## KŪLIA I KA NUʻU

Talk to your clients about why you work with certain professionals or with an established alliance. Ensure they understand that bringing in another specialist isn't a reflection of anything lacking on your part, because no one advisor can know everything about every detail of the many facets of banking, insurance, investments, tax, and the law. To do your best for them, you're focusing on them and the financial plan you've discussed that will give them what they're looking for in life. To deliver the best plan possible, they'll want you to introduce and engage with other advisors you trust who have the expertise and the products they need.

Reassure them that you will never simply hand them off to another advisor and that you'll share the necessary details about their wealth management goals to align your actions with theirs and deliver more in doing so. Finally, remind them that you are their lead advisor and will be with them throughout their journey, no matter whom else you've introduced them to from your collaborative.

# 10

# BECOMING AN ALOHA ADVISOR

Remember Hannah, the teacher from chapter 2? She didn't feel good about selling insurance because she didn't understand the value of what she provided to her clients. She'd never delivered a death benefit and seen the difference it makes for people in their most challenging moments in life.

Hannah began to believe in what she was doing and became very good at it. I'd love to tell you that Hannah went on to do wonderful things in this business. Unfortunately, once she started earning a good income, she became more ambitious. She suddenly left us to join a firm that promised her sexier financial strategies along with higher compensation. What Hannah did not know was that this company engaged in strategies that would prove unlawful, and it did not turn out well for them.

Too often advisors start off with good intentions. I taught Hannah how to build trust with her clients, and she became very successful at doing so. She wanted more. She forgot about what was important to people and focused on how much money she could make through structured products and services that did not necessarily serve her clients' best interests. She forgot about the importance of sharing with love, Aloha; of having gratitude, Mahalo; and of doing the right thing, Pono. She lost her way and failed to treat others like family, Ohana.

## REDEFINING SUCCESS

This happens all too often. An advisor starts off doing good, and then they give in to the greed factor, as they find themselves doing well and believe themselves entitled to even more. This isn't to say they end up in illegal business (like Hannah did). Still, the way they do business changes. An advisor who makes a lot of money focusing on the product, the sale, and themselves seldom seeks to try something else. They feel that the money is their only measure of success, and so there is no reason to do things differently.

As discussed in chapter 2, financial advisors are often trained in this manner. When you join a big investment firm, you're expected to introduce people to buy products offered through your firm and to do so in great volume. It's understandably the same with insurance companies. Once you sign on, you agree to sell whatever they offer. The top trainers at these companies continuously remind you to ask your prospects more questions, and they're right about that. But their intentions aren't always in line with mine. Often, questions are leading in nature, created to manipulate and disturb people into buying something. Truth be told, that's how I initially found financial success.

A lot of advisors make a lot of money this way. Some even convince themselves that asking disturbing questions is the only acceptable and most meaningful method for doing what's best for their clients. I think they're kidding themselves. If you're finding success through these kinds of techniques, why would you change? Why change the nature of your questions? For me, advisors who are making a lot of money this way and who can see themselves earning much more if they continue to be even sharper and more impactful with their leading questions are the most difficult people to encourage to make the change.

This isn't to say that I avoid addressing situations with my prospects and clients that might be disturbing. I talk to them about real life and ask them questions to discover what's important about what happens to the things they care about, such as their assets and the like, when it hits them. Sometimes that brings us down a disturbing path, as they venture into considering the possible death of a spouse or their very own. They might share their thoughts and plans for their aging parents or their growing children. What's important about what they wish to happen as they chase their hopes and face life's realities is always of importance to discuss. Just not in a disturbing way that "scares" them into action. We need to get everything on the table, to think clearly and design a financial plan together that addresses their concerns in a sensitive, caring way. We talk about what's truly important about these realities—how they'll be affected when life "happens to them" and what they can do now to manage it so that their plans will be fulfilled even when it does.

When I help people in this way, the reaction is positive. In fact, people usually take a more assertive role in our conversations when they realize just *how* important these matters are to them. They don't want to step lightly around them. They prefer to meet them head on and know their plans will go uncompromised when they occur. Someone who just spent four years taking care of his grandmother may want to know what he could do *now* so that caring for his mother as she ages won't lead to that same burdensome fate.

Manipulating people isn't sharing Aloha. It's not sharing the love, and it's not showing gratitude for the people in your life, like Mahalo. Manipulating people isn't Ohana—it's not treating people like family. It's definitely not Pono—doing the right thing. I find little righteousness in disturbing people in order to make a sale.

I question the intentions of advisors who focus on making sales specifically with leading questions that disturb prospects. "Do you intend to help this person, or do you intend to sell them something?" One could argue that this is what it comes down to. Most say that they intend to do both. Then they realize that all they have is an eight of clubs that they need to get rid of to be successful. If that's the case, how can they do anything more effective than asking leading questions to get to that outcome? They will never learn what the person in front of them really cares about, and it is highly doubtful that they'll do what's possible to help that person create a more fulfilled life for themselves. If you begin to rely only on tactics like this, ask yourself if you're manipulating your prospect's emotions to help them live a more fulfilled life or for you to live yours.

I'm not saying that leading questions should never be posed. Occasionally, a leading question is the quickest way to make a point to a person who is struggling with a concept, so if a question helps them get there, I'll ask it. My intention isn't to influence; it's to enlighten. There's a difference.

Beyond the ethical dilemma of working with people this way, you could miss out on the real opportunity. You never get to learn what the person is looking for, and there's a great chance that you could deliver that thing they're looking for to them. You basically end up shortchanging your client and yourself in the process. Still, it's difficult to convince an advisor who's making a lot of money doing it "their way" of this fact.

If you carry the kind of moral compass that points you toward righteousness and doing good for your clients with Pono, then you might find it easier to change your ways. Without that inner voice yelling at you to find a better way for you and your clients, it's difficult to encourage yourself to adopt a different way of financial advising when you're finding monetary success, even though doing so may give you access to even greater rewards.

## WHAT KIND OF ADVISOR DO YOU WANT TO BE?

The last thing I thought I'd do for a living was doing what my title says that I'm doing today. I didn't want to become a financial advisor because I thought everyone in it was a salesperson. That was a bad thing to me. I thought salespeople lived off the backs of people, and I wanted to be a person who took care of people.

Are you happy with your current situation? Are you happy with the kind of advisor you are today? Are you the financial advisor that you always wanted to be? Take a hard look at yourself in the mirror and see how you feel about that person staring back at you. Record yourself speaking with prospects and play it back to yourself. Are the words you hear those from the kind of person you'd want to be around? Is it the kind of person you'd want guiding and managing your financial plan?

Way back when I was just starting out, I used to listen to cassette tapes in my car. I played them on my way to meet with prospects and clients. The narrator had a lot of ideas about how to close sales, and I tried them, and they worked. Recently, I listened to one of those tapes again. I couldn't believe what I was hearing. The speaker's words were incredibly impactful, and I could see how using his techniques would resonate with clients. Unfortunately, they did not represent the kind of person I am now, or who I want to be. It's humbling to know how I aspired to be that very kind of advisor I now help others avoid becoming.

There are many methods, concepts, and techniques I've learned over the years that I haven't abandoned. I learned a lot about products and people and how to communicate better to make my points more resonant. I learned a lot about sales. You've probably learned a lot, too, and you don't have to abandon all that to become an Aloha Advisor.

You probably have a lot in your head that aligns very well here, so don't think you have to change everything you're doing. There are sales concepts that still apply and remain helpful tools. There are lessons you've taught your clients that you should continue teaching. Even leading questions at times are client-worthy to call upon.

Sometimes you can do everything right by a person, and they still find themselves stuck in neutral, unable to move forward with what's clearly a most important and agreed upon next step. If you have something to get them over the hump, and you're truly acting in their best interest, then do them and yourself a favor. Use it.

I do this and, when I do, I usually do it on purpose and with purpose. Sometimes it's a last resort. Regardless, you'll know when to do so. Sometimes it's to save people from themselves. For example, I have a client who's enamored by the glitz and bling of gems. Whenever he's got a little time and a little cash, he buys loose gems online or through one of those infomercial-type TV channels. He's convinced that one of these days he's going to find a gem worth much more than he paid in one of those batches.

This guy constantly told me how important it was that he buy life and disability insurance to be there to potentially replace his income and take care of his dependent wife and child in case life happened to him. Somehow, he could never find the money to pay for it. I told him a story, and it's a story I conjured a long time ago. It was far from a last resort. I cared about this guy and I could see that he was throwing his money away instead of taking care of what was truly important to him. He was full of contradiction, and that needed confronting.

I told him about a guy who had an ATM that spit out $8,000 every month. This was enough to cover all the basics in his life, so as long as the ATM worked, he was fine. His only worries were that the ATM might stop working for a short time, and that it might break down altogether. Of course, knowing this, he purchased a maintenance agreement that would get it fixed or replaced should either happen to his ATM.

Of course he would. It's logical and practical to do. When we strip ourselves of everything we are as people, other than our financial contributions to ourselves and those who depend upon us, we begin to resemble that ATM. We can become disabled due to sickness or injury. We will die. When either happens, our ability to earn and provide income for ourselves and those who depend upon us becomes threatened at the least and totally lost at the worst. Life happens, and we can break down temporarily or altogether. "Maintenance agreements for us breadwinners are called disability insurance and life insurance," I told him. "If you, your family's ATM, break down, the policies ensure the money to fix or replace it so that $8,000 a month will always be there."

I wasn't trying to scare the guy. I was trying to make a point. He wasn't connecting the dots for himself enough to realize that keeping the family ATM working was more important than gambling on TV gems to those most important to him.

### YOU'VE DONE WELL SO FAR

You've probably been in this business for a while. If this is true, then you've already beaten the odds. Like I mentioned earlier, 86 percent of people who do what we do are out of the business within three years. But here you are, in the upper 14 percent that either have found success or are well on their way to success. Congratulations!

Now you have *another* way to find success. You can understand what people want in their lives and make an impact on those things that mean the most to them. You can continue to use the powerful concepts that have led you to the success you currently enjoy. You can meet people with your open heart and quiet mind, without judgment, and appreciate them for who they are and what they care about. You don't have to give up everything you know to do this; it's simply a different approach from a different place.

You may be surprised by how much happier you'll be doing it

this way. Let go of all judgment toward your clients and stop imposing your opinions on them, in your head and out loud. Stop presuming to know people before you actually get to know them, because you can't know a person without asking them questions and finding out what matters to them. The temptation to fill in what you don't know about a person, to simply assume, can be overwhelming. Once you stop doing that and seek to learn their truth, you may find yourself enjoying them and their unique perspectives on life even more than you thought.

Have you ever eaten noodles in a traditional Asian restaurant? Were people there slurping their noodles? Were you thinking that these people were being rude? Perhaps you made that judgment before arming yourself with the proper information. Some say that it's customary to slurp noodles in Asia because that's how you get the broth into your mouth along with the noodles. It tastes better that way. Others say that failing to slurp your noodles tells the chef that their dish isn't tasty enough. Whatever the reason, slurping noodles in Asia is the right thing to do, especially when it comes to noodles in soup or ramen. In the United States, people who slurp their noodles are thought to be rude. Could it be that the people who judge them just don't have enough information?

If you meet with a person and they're slurping their noodles or doing something that doesn't fit your expectations, withhold your judgment. Get to know the person. Ask them questions. You'll likely learn something new when you do.

## TEACHING PEOPLE TO BE BETTER CLIENTS

Years ago, an article I wrote about disability insurance and reverse mortgages was published in a magazine for seniors. It told the story of a man in a wheelchair who was at the mall speaking with this young woman. The man's neighbors happened to see him and assumed he was flirting with the girl. They were friends of his wife, and what they didn't know was that the man was asking the woman for help picking out a dress for his wife as a gift. The women gossiped away. The message was basically that things aren't always as they appear.

A mom read the story and sent it to her daughter and son-in-law. She wanted them to visit with me and set up disability insurance plans for themselves and a reverse mortgage for her.

I wrote the article to encourage people to get the facts about reverse mortgages before buying into one, not necessarily to sell them. I wanted people to ask me about them so they could educate themselves. Reverse mortgages aren't right for everyone or every circumstance, nor is anything else, for that matter. Some advisors believe that they're never the right answer. Whatever the product, it needs to be the right fit, and it needs to be structured properly to maximize its ultimate benefit to a person.

I needed to find out what was important to this couple and their mother about this particular financial move. As it turned out, Mom needed money for another one of her children.

I could have done what they asked. Instead, I asked them if they wanted my professional advice. They did.

"Professionally speaking," I told them, "I can help get this done for you. My advice is to also consider other alternatives among the many that may prove better for your mom's situation."

They were glad to hear that there were other strategies to consider, and I was happy to step them through several better options than what they *thought* best to get the job done.

In a different publication, I wrote about a technique commonly referred to as pension maximization, where an individual opts to receive their entire pension while they're alive instead of leaving the remainder, after death, to their joint survivor, their spouse. This increases their monthly payout and some of the additional funds they receive—say, 60 percent of them—are then diverted into a life insurance plan with the spouse as the beneficiary to its benefits.

In some situations, this plan works well. Again, each individual and situation is unique, so it's not always a good idea to implement for some. Again, someone read the article and passed it on to a friend, who, along with his wife, came to see me. They wanted me to set them up in a pension maximization plan.

I listened to the couple, and then I talked to them about what I do and how I do it. I asked them about what was important to them and why, and I broadened the conversation beyond retirement. We talked about why they needed the additional cash flow later in their lives, and I discovered they had children and were concerned about them, too. It would have been very easy for me to follow their request and sell them a couple of life insurance policies aimed much further down the road.

The more I learned about these people, the more apparent it became that there were more important options for them to consider and immediately prioritize. In the end, they asked me to help them with their retirement plans, their income protection plans, and their estate plan. They eagerly introduced me to other couples they knew.

Instead of simply completing transactions and earning fees and commissions, I secured new, trusting clients for life, and that's because I was able to help them get what they really wanted. I ended up with advocates who promoted me to their families and friends and who learned that they shouldn't accept the first thing that's offered to them.

People have been conditioned by our efforts and expect to be sold. They're surrounded by marketing and sales in their everyday lives, and they expect the same treatment from people they meet with when they want something. You can teach them to expect more from their advisors.

When your prospects begin telling you about themselves, your mind may immediately jump to what you think is the "solution" to what they raise as their concern or hope. You'll want to tell them all about it. It feels like the hottest of leads that you need to turn into a sale as quickly as possible. You want to be their hero. You want to tell them that you have the answer for them. Yet, at this very moment, you're better advised to leave that lead alone.

When you get that urge, stay silent and let them keep talking. Ask. Listen. Learn. Repeat. There's usually a lot more going on than what they first tell you.

Think of it like this. Say you have a sore toe. You immediately think there's something wrong with your toe, so you put some cream on it. It still hurts, so you cover it with a Band-Aid. The next day your toe is throbbing and turning colors, so you wrap your whole foot in an ACE bandage. That night, the pain is so bad that you finally go to the emergency room. The doctor looks at you and asks, "What are you doing walking around with a broken leg?" That's right—you broke your leg and have been walking funny, and your toe's rubbing the top of your shoe. That's why it hurts.

You can't expect people to tell you about their broken legs. You can't even expect them to tell you about their sore toes. They may not even know about them. This is why we purposefully ask, listen, and learn and continue to discover to ensure that we do know what's going on in that person's life and the origin of their pain.

Let people take you on their life's journey. It's how both you and they discover what's sincerely important to them. After they talk about the toe, and the foot, and the knee, and a host of other things, they'll eventually get to the root cause of what's worrying them—that thing they care so much about that they overcame their fear of visiting with a financial services salesperson and came to you, a financial advisor, to understand and appreciate them for who they are and where they are and to help them achieve what they wish to achieve with what they have to do so. They came to you for help.

When you get to that point with a person, their picture comes alive. It becomes vivid. You should be able to repeat all that they've shared with you and ultimately say to them, "This is what I understand is of importance in your life, and this is what needs to happen to make you happy." If they agree that this is it—achieving all of this will make them happy—then you're there. And when you lead them toward that promised place, they'll follow you anywhere, and they should.

It's time for you to move on to the next step: fact finding.

Once you know what your prospects want, you must go on a fact-finding mission to discover what they have relative to what they hope to achieve. I generally prefer my staff handle this process. Removing myself keeps it more objective, and I'm able to learn much more during my clarification and confirmation discussion that follows. The information is loaded into a database where I can view and assess what they have and how best to use what they have to get them what they desire.

These days many feel better when they're directly involved and often prefer to even enter their information for themselves. Regardless of how information is gathered, prospective clients, staff, and I ultimately review all inputs before formal plans are derived and executed. The advantage to this is I'm not judging them while they're giving me this information. My mind isn't going to products. I'm able to look at their entire financial situation and get the big picture, which prevents me from making siloed decisions about what they need to do to get what they want.

When I look at a prospect's situation, I sometimes find places where they need the advice of a specialist, and that's when I look to my collaborative. Viewing the data on my own, instead of with prospects, allows me to see it with an unbiased eye so I can consider and ask better questions of what they've implemented and offer them better options to meet their goals. And as you already know, sometimes those options are represented through others outside of my organization.

## KŪLIA I KA NU'U

Remember why you got into this business in the first place. Think about what drives you in this business now. Are you happy with what your business is delivering? Do you like what you do and how you do it? If you want to change, you can start today with subtle changes.

Meet with people and see them as people instead of prospects or soon-to-be clients. Practice asking questions and don't let your mind jump to products. In fact, don't talk about your products at all. Get the full picture of what they desire in their lives. Start with the end in mind. Then, learn where they are relative to where they wish to go with proper fact finding. Do all this before you even start thinking about products, even if they tell you they have one in mind for themselves and per-haps even more so when they do. Tell them you can talk to them about that one thing they think they need, and that it would be in their best interest to demand more from you.

# GETTING TO THE END ZONE

In the United States, the point of entry for many financial advisors in search of clients of substance is the estate planning attorney. The reason behind this is that, typically, this type of attorney is the first professional a prospect with significant assets seeks out for financial management-related structural advice and counsel, especially when it comes to issues centered on transferring their wealth. Estate planning attorneys are key to financial advisors who are prepared to provide the most appropriate financial products behind their chosen legal structures. These attorneys often play the role of lead advisor.

I learned that this isn't necessarily the case in other countries. In Japan, for example, lawyers—including estate or wealth transfer planning attorneys—while sought for their professional counsel, are often poorly positioned like transactional *salespeople*. While salespeople provide an important service in many industries, informed wealth management advice that serves the interests of an individual requires much more than the facilitation of transactions. Prospects seeking assistance with their finances in this manner, then, do not typically view their attorneys as skilled professionals acting as mentors or guides. They view them as people who simply follow their (often uninformed) instructions. In fact, looking closer at the situation in Japan and in some other countries, I realized that *most* practitioners within the sectors of the wealth management profession are disappointingly viewed as salespeople, often purely transaction-based or promoting specific concepts as their general craft: life insurance agents, investment advisors, private bankers, tax advisors, attorneys, and the like.

My journey to find the ideal point of entry in Japan circled all of these professionals and eventually led me to that country's tax advisors and consulting firms. These people weren't viewed as salespeople. They were called and looked up to as *sensei*, "teacher" in Japanese. More importantly, they didn't feel threatened by me, as I was clearly not a competitor. I wasn't even from their country. Of course, our businesses operated in other countries and, given Japan's decidedly industry-protection-centered regulatory environment, we could only help support specific communities within Japan to which our company's registration allowed, and the product offerings could only come from the one company from the United States with legal standing at the time in Japan. This was without regard to the ultimate benefit to residents of their country. So when a situation called for a product and service from a firm outside of their country without legal standing, no solicitation of any kind could take place. This is customary in many parts of the world.

Because of this, the only way a regulated company or individual such as a tax firm or tax advisor could help their clients obtain opportunities from outside their country was to find ways to coordinate with those they could trust from these outside jurisdictions and then let their clients go on their own to consider and potentially execute for their benefit. Most were happy and willing to enjoy reviewing the tax consequences and total result opportunities that their clients found through strategies from abroad. Some introduced me to their clients, confident that I'd provide a service that complemented, rather than detracted from, their own. It was (and still is) an easy process for any introducing professional: all that's needed is for them to make the introduction to me and leave. In most jurisdictions, that's all they're allowed to do anyway. Once they do, I work with their clients in the same way I work with those that live in America, finding out what's important to them. Sharing Aloha. Despite the cultural differences and, in many cases, the language barrier, my prospects from outside of the United States respond in the same way as their American counterparts. They're happy to share what is most important to them and all that might lead to their idea of a fulfilled life.

Early on, I learned something else unique to these prospects, and I found it to be true in several other countries: they diverged from Americans when it came to transparently divulging current holdings. During our conversations of purposeful discovery, I often uncovered details of their finances that they hadn't shared with their tax advisor—the very person who had introduced us! I found that it was, and still is, common for clients of substantial wealth to retain several advisors, tax and otherwise, none of whom had the big picture of the person's financial situation. That was the case for one individual I was called on to assist. He retained *three* tax advisors, none of whom had a complete understanding of the man's assets, cash flow, and other financial details.

This was (and is) intentional—many of the people I meet don't want any one person to know their business and personal holdings in totality, how they're owned, and whom they might benefit. Often, they might call on a tax advisor to handle the property they own, a second advisor for their wife and children, and a third tax advisor for the things they're doing for someone else—sometimes even for their girlfriend and the family they share together. Each culture has its own unique personality.

The bottom line is that for me to serve this new prospect introduced by one of his tax advisors to the best of my ability, I had to convince him to share everything with me or with *someone* who had full knowledge—if not access—to all of his finances. That's no small task when you consider the cultural shaping during the man's life that insists he keep his financial information segmented and discrete. At the very least, I believed that he should engage a tax professional or other key advisor he trusted to provide him with overarching advice on his entire financial situation or at least effectively understand and articulate his overall goals and desires. By limiting what he shared with each of his advisors, he was unintentionally inviting compromise and contradiction in financial guidance that could lead to poorly constructed, uncoordinated strategies, potentially jeopardizing his planned outcomes. Situations such as this are common, and they tend to worsen as clients age.

My preference is for people to rely on a lead advisor or a team of advisors who know the individual's entire financial situation, someone they trust implicitly to execute on their behalf.

While I believe that's an imperative, some people prefer to

work with many advisors, each of whom is privy to limited information about the person's financial information. If it's coordinated and translates to deliver what the client wants, then it's true that one could argue that type of setup works. I just don't find it ideal. In the case of the person who had three tax advisors, there's little doubt that he would have achieved a better outcome had he chosen one tax advisor with a keen understanding and appreciation of all assets held and what was of importance to him relative to them.

Still, some people don't like working that way. They prefer to call upon individual advisors for different pockets of their lives.

## PROSPECTS NEED TO PUSH THE JOURNEY

If you've established trust with a person, it's to their benefit to share openly with you. Trust is important, of course, because if they can't trust you to do what's in their best interest, they shouldn't be sharing with you anyway.

Rather than hold back and expect advisors to press the financial journey forward, prospects should be the ones doing the pushing. If they truly want to be understood, they're best served to tell me what I need to know. This is how they push the journey forward—by telling me more and more so we can both get to the heart of what matters most to them *beyond* the money, the assets, the products, and the services.

It's necessary that they do this, because people naturally come with built-in biases and see their situation from a different perspective than I can. Assets and cash flow and how they're arranged are key factors in any financial plan, and my prospects and I agree in that respect.

No matter what a prospect defines as their fulfilled life, you can help them move closer to it regardless of their balance sheet. If you focus on the money from the start, which is what your prospects are likely to do, you threaten to limit your thinking. They know what they own and already worked through the exercise of deciding what's financially out of reach for them. They have done this with limited knowledge, though, because they're not a financial expert like you.

When prospects think this way, they're already considering the products they believe they need and can afford. It's up to you to get them out of this way of thinking, and that's because you can do better for them than what they have decided they can do for themselves—and you will, *once they let you.*

## BEYOND DOLLARS AND CENTS

When I approach a suspect or meet with a prospect or client, I rarely start the conversation with a dollar amount or ask for a budget. If someone goes there, it's usually because they've seen a salesperson and a product and have established a budget for it from what they believe is their discretionary cash flow. That's fine. Prospects may have a budget and a goal in mind for that budget, and they want me to make a transaction for them. As an Aloha Advisor, rather than immediately moving forward with their request, I'd want to know more. I'm not a salesperson dealing in commodities, and I want to ensure that what I'm doing for this person is in their best interest.

People tend to make a lot of assumptions when it comes to figuring out their finances on their own. The typical person doesn't understand how to adequately prepare for retirement. They don't know how much money they need to be saving today and which financial products to lean on to enjoy a fulfilled life now and in the future. They don't know what to do to ensure the quality of life they desire after they stop working. Many people don't know how much life insurance is needed to replace their income, or how they'll prepare to leave enough money to care for their children and meet the goals they have for them should life happen to them along the way. They may not be considering that whatever they leave to their kids will probably sit for many years, so there's a lot of growth left for them to manage, too. There's a whole lot to consider, and unless the money part is put aside and they talk to you about what they really want, you won't be able to do the best job for them. You're basically allowing them to turn you into a salesperson looking to make a sale.

Why would you do this? They're not the expert—you are. As they begin to learn from you, they'll be surprised by all you teach them and grateful that you put the money discussion aside and focused on them instead.

When I put the transaction request aside and begin asking questions about what's important to a person, I usually hear, "I've never really thought about that." There's a lot that people don't think about. People of significant means don't think about all that they've built over their lifetimes and what's going to happen to it when they pass on. Business owners don't consider what will happen to their companies once they're gone. They often fail to discuss what to do with their business at their passing with their spouse or children. It seems natural for people to derive detailed plans for these things of such great importance; most do not. Many don't think that broadly, or that deeply, or that far ahead about what's most important to them when all is said and done. They're busy, and instead of the ultimate big picture, they're usually focused on what's next.

## THE CLIENT CONSULTATIVE METHOD

The traditional journey of discovery begins with fact-finding. The advisor questions a prospect to find out what they own and then comes up with a plan of action to get the most out of those holdings, potentially focused on what they want or where they want to be.

The reality is if you start there, you're in the wrong place. The facts are the biases and the limiters. The facts can even keep you from moving effectively forward. Oftentimes, prospects' facts paralyze advisors because we don't know what to do with them once we have them—never mind all the new ones constantly emerging. Beginning with the facts can lead the focus toward the challenges of life rather than its possibilities. It's why I always seek to start with the end in mind.

## DIG DEEP, SEEK THE TRUTH, AND AVOID SOUR GRAPES

My friends and colleagues will tell you that I love wine, and that my favorite wine is typically the one in the glass in front of me. Don't get me wrong, I have my preferences. Yes, when it comes to fermented grape juice, I can be a bit of a snob. Still, I'm not much of a connoisseur. I'm really more of a consumer. So please forgive me as I share my parallel between fine wine and my method of interviewing.

You see, my understanding is that great wine comes from grapes that are high in sugar. This may be best reflected in grapes grown in extreme temperatures of hot days and cold nights—extreme enough to produce the high sugar content yet not so hot or cold as to kill the grapes. This kind of environment makes the West Coast of North America—Napa Valley and the Central Coast of California, the Willamette Valley in Oregon, and Yakima and the Columbia River Valley of Washington—such wonderfully hopeful regions to harvest proper fruit.

I believe it's similar when it comes to financial planning. The best interviews involve the extremes of hot and cold that aren't so hot or cold as to kill the discussion or cripple your relationship. In the financial planning interview, I believe the heat is lit during the emotion-based discovery process, as people share from the heart. The cold comes with the logical delivery of facts, circumstances, and plans for your prospects' consideration and potential actions. The combination is like enjoying the finest of wine.

And I now realize it goes even further than that. During a visit to a winery that delivers fantastic zinfandels, I was taught a fascinating lesson. I was asked, "Which type of soil produces the tastiest grapes, poor soil or rich soil?" I quickly answered, "Rich soil!" Of course, I was wrong. In a nutshell, I learned that over the long term, grapes grown in poorer soil can produce better grapes leading to better wines. Rich topsoil makes it easy for grape vines to find nutrients near the surface. The roots don't need to dig and fight for their food. Well, I also learned that, over time, the sturdiest vines tend to produce the best-tasting grapes. The sturdier vines that produce these grapes are represented by vines with roots that are well entrenched deep below the surface. Apparently, the fewer nutrients found at the top, the deeper the roots dig to find the source of nutrition needed. The further they dig, the sturdier the vine and the better the grapes. They're digging until they find their life source, their nutrition—and that feeds the juicy grapes that hang above it all.

Much the same is true when it comes to discovering our prospects' core values within the interview process…we're seeking to find their life source—the things they really care about, find of most importance, and sincerely want to make reality. Our objective is to go far beyond the surface and dive deep. And when we do that, we discover what the person sincerely values and finds of value, which will facilitate the following:

- Help them articulate their values to you and themselves *and allow you to*
- Earn trust on purpose and with purpose *by*
- Asking discovery questions as part of a conversation. *You'll then*
- Confirm what you discovered *and*
- Begin the fact-finding process *that will ultimately*
- Provide alternative plans of action that address what your prospect really cares about.

# Client Consultative Methodology

The client consultative method takes your prospect from the Red Zone through Green Fields to the open Blue Ocean.

## TO GET TO THE END ZONE, START IN THE RED ZONE

Imagine you're the star quarterback, and it's the end of the fourth quarter at the Super Bowl. You're on the losing end of a twenty-four to twenty score with just two seconds left to play. You stare down the field toward the end zone. That's where you'll need a perfect Hail Mary pass, your one last heave of the football, to score and win the game. You squint your eyes, and the end zone seems so far away. All your receivers are tiny bumps on the horizon. You're never going to get the ball all the way down there because you haven't *positioned* yourself to get it there. You're not in the red zone.

In case you need a quick refresher on American football: teams must make their way past the goal line and into the end zone to score. When they get within twenty yards of the goal line, they're in what's called the "red zone." Teams try to position themselves for the best opportunity to score. They want to be in that red zone—especially when it comes down to the wire and being in or out of that zone usually leads to a team winning or losing the game.

In wealth management, there's another Red Zone where you, the financial advisor, must position yourself to "score"— moving a suspect or prospect to client status. The Red Zone is where you purposefully build trust with your prospect, which positions you to make the greatest impact on the relationship.

Top advisors begin each new relationship in the Red Zone, creating that trust and setting themselves up to score *before* attempting to do so. Traditional financial advising methods, however, tend to skip the effort to position themselves within this zone. Instead, many advisors assume the prospect already trusts them or will come to trust them, and they go directly into what I call the Green Fields by attempting to collect and work on the facts.

The problem is that by skipping the Red Zone, your prospect may not yet trust you enough to give you the green light to move forward and dig into all the facts of their financials. I'm mixing metaphors here, yet I think you get the picture: you just ran the red light and are careening through the Green Fields without permission. You may think you're doing a great job, gathering all those facts, when in fact you're only getting part of your prospect's story. They don't know you and whether to trust you, and they have not given you permission to really know them factually or emotionally.

Get to know people and make your way to the Red Zone by discovering what their hopes are first. People want hope. It's perhaps the most significant of wants. Hope can serve as an elixir for life and living. People don't only want hope; they need it. Hope is what keeps us going, reaching for more, striving to achieve whatever it is we find of importance to bring to life what isn't so in our lives today. We want to believe there is a better life ahead for us. People want more for their kids, their grandchildren, their spouses, and themselves, yet they may never have articulated what that means. I start there with people—with hope.

Beyond the facts and the challenges, I want to understand the person in front of me and know what they truly value and hope for. What's their reason for being, what's deep down in their core, what's driving them, what do they live for, and what are they even willing to die for? You can't know that by focusing on only the facts.

Understanding your prospects is how you build trust, and it doesn't come by simply spending time with them—it's what you *do* in that time. It's what you talk about—the questions you ask and what they tell you. It's what you learn about them. Listen carefully to understand them and learn what they care most about. That's crucial.

Getting into the Red Zone with a person is a precious thing. The trust and vulnerability involved is similar to a great doctor-patient relationship. Imagine that you, as the patient, have a health issue going on. You make an appointment with your doctor, the guy you've been going to for twenty years. He knows your whole history, has seen you naked dozens of times, and understands everything about every personal, private, embarrassing, sensitive, and just plain boring health issue you've had over the past few decades. You're totally comfortable seeing him again. He knows you. You get into the examination room, strip down, put on that paper smock with the tie in the back, and wait for your old pal the doctor to walk in. Except your doctor isn't available today, and in walks a doctor whom you've never seen before.

You're mortified. You don't know this young woman—have never even seen her, never mind been to the Red Zone with her. You don't trust her and have no plans whatsoever to bare your soul (or anything else) to her. Where is *your* doctor, the one you know and trust? He's the person you want to talk to, the only person you'll ever want to talk to about what's going on with your health.

This is what it's like once you get into the Red Zone with a prospect. You essentially strip the person down, not physically—you're going *deeper*. You get to their soul and discover what moves them—what makes them tick. What makes them get out of bed in the morning and drives them to take action to ensure that what matters financially to them most is identified, accounted for, and fulfilled. Once I get to that point with a person, they want to see me *and no one else every time*. They're comfortable with me, and they know and trust me. Getting to that point was necessary for us to work best together, and they do not want to repeat the process with another advisor.

Part of building trust in the Red Zone is keeping my personal opinions and biases to myself—they have no place in this conversation. Knowing my prospects and accepting them, regardless of how much our own opinions align or differ, is how I create trust on purpose. Once they know that I understand what they desire, and I want to help them get it, they can decide whether they want to move forward to make it happen or not.

If I understand and appreciate what they're telling me and I articulate their words back to them in a way that reflects how they really feel, they'll want to move forward. There are few questions and little confusion about what they want and what I intend to focus on for them. They see that we're aligned in our understanding of what they care to make happen. This is what happens in the Red Zone.

Skipping over the Red Zone means you skipped the most critical part of the process, where you build a solid foundation with your prospective client by taking the time to understand the person, and perhaps even more importantly, you give them the opportunity to *believe* you understand them. If they don't believe you understand them, you haven't successfully and purposefully developed that trust. Building trust on purpose, rather than expecting it to happen naturally, is the best way I've found to move a person from suspect to prospect to client to advocate. An advocate who introduces people to *you*.

Get yourself in that Red Zone. Plant yourself there and get comfortable. Once you're solidly positioned in the Red Zone, you *will* score. You'll get the green light into the Green Fields, make it to the end zone, and eventually enjoy all that open Blue Ocean of opportunity ahead.

## FROM RED ZONE TO GREEN FIELDS

The Green Fields are where you receive agreement from your prospect to gather facts—to learn what they hold and how they're positioned and to know everything about the "green" they own—their assets. This is where you gather all the details of their situation so you can develop a plan for them to implement that helps them achieve what they shared with you in the Red Zone.

Understanding the prospect's real wants and the complete facts of their situation gives me the information I need to design options for them to make their wishes a reality. At this point, I let the person know that I'm going to gather facts about their current situation and develop a plan for them that satisfies or exceeds the wants they expressed to me. Typically, I say something like, "I'll be sharing different ways to get you on a better track to meeting your hopes. If you should find my ideas of value, I hope that I can expect you to implement the products and services behind these plans we create for you through me. Does this work for you?"

With the foundation of trust and the person's approval to move forward in place, you can begin uncovering their facts. Fact-finding at this point will be more fruitful due to your diligence in the Red Zone. The person will be willing to share more information with you about their situation. They realize that it's self-serving for them to do so.

Understanding the facts about a prospect is a rigorous process, and it's not just about numbers. There are feelings involved, too, so I dig deep to discover how the person feels about things and uncover any assumptions they're making based on their beliefs. For example, they may feel a certain way about what they currently hold in their portfolio, the effects of inflation, or their experiences with stock market volatility; how they feel about those issues is important to understand and appreciate.

As you already know, the data part of fact-finding is one part of the process that I trust to my staff, and some prospects prefer to provide this information themselves, through a secure website. However they choose to share and access their financial information, it's still secondary to understanding what they want—their hopes, dreams, and desires.

You can charge a fee for the plan you create if you like, or you can opt to not charge for it and hope that your prospect indeed becomes your client and agrees to move forward with you. Some advisors let the prospect know up front that there is a fee for the plan, and they will either discount or waive the fee if they're called upon to implement the plan. Then they earn their fees and commissions in that way. When it comes to fees and commissions, there are many variations to consider as each methodology comes with its unique set of advantages and benefits. Choose well.

On a few occasions of which I'm aware, an advisor took the plan we derived and made tens of thousands of dollars off my work. It can happen. That's not enough to make me change my method, because in the long run, I'm able to do more good and do better for more clients my way than if I charged them up front for the plan or demanded they work only with me. Regardless of what happens, I choose to move forward with my values intact. As long as I behave with Pono, doing right by my prospects and clients, I know that I'm on the right path.

As I develop a plan, typically with several alternative paths to reach the person's goals, I continue to assess and analyze their current situation relative to those goals. I check in with the person along the way to ensure we're still on the right path, too. They've bared their soul to me and to themselves, figuring out what will make them happy, and I've designed several ways to make it happen for them. Now I can present plan alternatives to this person knowing that I've done everything the way I should, the way I'd want another advisor to do it for me. By this point, it's logical to assume that should the person decide that any one of the alternatives I've designed works for them and decide to move forward, they'll do so with me.

At this point, why wouldn't they want to move forward? With our focus on all that's important to them, there are seldom more questions. If there are, don't misinterpret them as objections. Objections are simply questions. Questions signal interest; they're requests for more information. Unless you lied to the person (in which case you're missing the whole point of Aloha financial advising), you have nothing to fear.

The person may ask how I get paid, and I tell them. It's not a secret—I have nothing to hide and no reason to avoid the question. I value the service I provide, and if I've done my job with the best intentions and to the best of my abilities, they do as well. Now the person is ready to receive my ideas and eager to learn how they can get where they want to be faster and more efficiently than whatever they're currently doing. Once they agree to act, and they almost always do, we enter the Blue Ocean. The open Blue Ocean is home to all the possibilities and opportunities available to your client!

## FINISH (AND START AGAIN) IN THE OPEN BLUE OCEAN

The Blue Ocean is where the plan is implemented and I monitor progress. It's when everything we've worked on together begins to come to life. Competitors fall away, and we face nothing except for the vast array of opportunities ahead of us. As I put my carefully designed plan into motion and my clients see how it moves them closer to getting what they're looking for in life, they thank me—often. And every time they thank me, I ask for a referral. I'll tell you more about this process in the conclusion. It's how the cycle closes and begins again and why I never worry about running out of great people to meet who appreciate my help and what I can do for them.

## KŪLIA I KA NU'U

Expect more from your prospects and clients and push them to expect more from you. They may come to you with a preconceived idea of what they want, and more than likely it's a product they think they need based on their limited knowledge and their budget.

They may want to talk to you about their assets or an immediate item of pressing concern. Tell them you want to talk to them about that and let them know that it may not be the deciding factor in their financial plan. That may surprise them initially, until you explain what you do and how you do it. Then they'll begin to understand.

Let them also know how important this is to you and how important it should be for them. Their financial plan can be life-changing, so they should be willing to take the time to step through your questions so you can learn what they desire and help you understand their definition of a fulfilled life.

# 12

# PONO PAYS

When people invest in things that bring them value, they rarely worry about whether someone's making money by providing it to them. The same is true in financial advising. Usually, they *want* you to make money. They certainly expect you to do so. If it doesn't compromise what they're getting, most will want you to get something in return, too.

When you're doing good for others and making money, what you earn takes on a different meaning. It's no longer a symbol of greed; it's proof of the good you've done. Generally, the more people I help achieve fulfilled lives, the more money I make, and the more I do to help those people achieve fulfilled lives, the more money I make.

I don't get overly caught up in fees and commissions. My prospects are typically satisfied with my opening comments and disclosures around how I get paid, and they rarely ask me about my compensation. Frankly, I believe that my prospects and clients would never ask me about compensation detail, even if I failed to provide the clarifying information that we advisors require ourselves to deliver. As long as I'm getting the job done and serving their interests, people tend to focus on themselves, their finances, and what they want their money to fund instead of worrying about how I'm being compensated. If they do ask for more details, I provide whatever additional information they seek on the subject.

Some advisors worry about that kind of transparency. I welcome it. People should be aware of the value we bring and why we receive the income we do for our services. Government regulations that force this kind of openness aren't anything to be afraid of—they're doing us a favor by getting it out there for individuals to recognize. The more they know about how we make money, the better they can appreciate the value of our services and the easier it is for us to do the right things for them.

Doing right by your clients allows them to accomplish more of those things of most importance to them and allows you to make more, too. That's something trusting clients understand and support.

Once your clients fully understand the value from their relationship with you, they'll be open to writing testimonials for you. They'll become your advocates. They'll talk about you in ways you could never talk about yourself. They'll refer the people they care about to you, because they want those people to enjoy the value you bring, and they'll want you to be successful, too. You'll attract more people like those you enjoy helping most who share similar core values. The goodness keeps coming, and the more good you do, the more you benefit.

## KŪLIA I KA NU'U

Being an Aloha Financial Advisor won't limit your ability to make money—it will unleash it. You'll feel good about doing it, and your clients will support it. Train yourself to look at making money in a different way. You don't earn it by winning a competition with your clients or competitors. You can make more money with Mahalo, by being grateful for your prospects, clients, and advocates and appreciating their unique approach to life. You can make more money with Ohana, by being honest and forthright with them and treating them like family. You can do it by doing the right thing, Pono, and by becoming more valuable to yourself and your clients, Imua. You can make more money by sharing Aloha.

Do good for your clients, and you will reap the rewards.

There is no shame in that. Celebrate it.

# PONO FOR THE PEOPLE

I wanted to open this chapter with a unique story about how doing good can serve your clients better. The trouble is this outcome is so common that it's not unique at all—it's the *norm*.

There's a reason for this: when you put yourself and whatever products and services you have to offer aside and focus on the person in front of you, you inspire them to discover a lot about themselves.

Let me explain how this works.

When I meet with a new prospect and ask them questions centered on what matters to them in life, the typical initial response I get is, "I don't know." They usually pause to think about it more, and they often tell me, "No one has ever asked me that before."

How is it that the advisors who met with this person in the past failed to discover what was important both generally and specifically about their money and how it relates to what matters in life to them? Even more fascinating and perhaps a bit concerning is how it is that this individual has never thought deeply about what matters to them within the context of their lives.

By asking your prospects these questions and encouraging them to consider their responses carefully and thoughtfully, you can empower them to identify the targets in their lives on which their focus should be aimed. This can take them in new directions. Instead of focusing on what's urgent, or what's expected, or what they've been made to believe should be important to them, they can change their focus and direct their lives toward what's *truly of most importance to them.*

Oftentimes, this experience is an epiphany for people. The difference between advising prospects and clients this way and advising them the traditional way can be dramatic when a prospective client comes to me for a second opinion. They've met with an advisor who told them they need to buy life insurance, or they need to open a Roth IRA, or they need to have a higher percentage of their investments in tax-deferred accounts, for example.

When a person comes to me with a financial decision in mind, I can easily sell them whatever they think it is that they need. That alone isn't doing the best I can do for that person. Instead, I listen to them, and then I ask them what was of importance to them that led them to their decision. What's important to them about purchasing that life insurance policy or investing into that Roth IRA or that taxable account? I listen to their answers, because there must be reasons driving these important decisions, and I want to know what they are.

During this process, I usually discover that there is something *more* important to them than whatever immediate issue they're trying to solve with this financial decision they've already made—this product they think they need.

People don't always know what they want simply because they haven't thought deeply enough about what would make them happy. Sometimes they do know and believe it isn't possible. Often, they don't bother addressing their wants because they're just not very knowledgeable about how to satisfy them. They may have conditioned themselves to lower their expectations and think within certain limits, and, of the varied options provided by their previous advisors, none were aimed and shaped to suit their specific situation.

Whatever the reason, asking your prospect questions, discovering what matters to them, and then helping them prioritize these things of importance is an eye-opening experience. It may show them that there's much more to consider and do than simply buy a new policy or make a new investment.

When you help someone realize all that's important in their lives and further identify, agree to, and commit to the prioritization of what's most important to do to achieve it, you perfectly position yourself to help them reach their goals. They'll be more grounded and in touch with their wants so they can communicate with you from a more authentic place, too. They'll see the strategies, and the products that you recommend behind the strategies, as vital to meeting their goals. They will know they need to secure them, and they'll help you help them do so. This allows you to do the utmost good for them.

## REARRANGING GOALS TO MATCH PRIORITIES

Whatever prospects tell me first is seldom the root of what it is we end up focusing on. This is so often the case that now I typically remind myself that what someone initially *tells* me is their issue is probably not the real issue at hand. They might think they have their priorities in order. Because they haven't fully explored them, they often overlook things or underestimate their importance. Like the example with the hurt toe, what they may want to talk to me about may be a symptom of a much bigger issue or goal or want they have. Once we get to the bottom of their unmet desires, we can begin to prioritize what's truly important to them.

When a person tells me that it's their children who are first and foremost to them when it comes to money, it's a must for us to explore that. What's important about what they provide to their children and how that affects their finances to them? I don't make assumptions because parents have different opinions about matters regarding their children. For instance, while parents typically want to help prepare their children to excel in life, not every parent believes the way to do that is by paying for college. Some parents believe in traditional higher education and others believe in trade schools, while other parents want their children to make their own ways in life. Instead of jumping to conclusions, if a parent expresses to me that they want to help their children prepare for life, I ask them what that means to them and what's important to provide to help them do so to them.

They might tell me they want their kids to go to college. Then it's vital that I learn what's important to them about the kind of college and the items we prepare for to properly fund their children's potential attendance. Some parents want their kids to go to an Ivy League school. Other parents want their children to attend a school that's close to where they live. Still other parents have no intention of paying for their kids to continue their education past high school. They have other goals that are a higher priority than paying for college, such as funding their retirement plan or traveling. They may simply philosophically believe it best for their children to make their own decisions and carve out their own unique paths.

If a prospect does want to establish plans focused on establishing funds necessary to pay for their kids' education, we talk about that, and the earlier the better. There's a tendency for people to focus on what they immediately want, so saving for college may seem less of a priority to them. If they carry high expectations for their kids to go to an expensive school, they shouldn't wait until the children are in high school to start thinking about how they're going to finance it. By then, they've missed out on precious years of potential financial growth.

This makes these conversations and our work to prioritize together of even greater importance. Suffering from a disabling injury or sickness, living too long, and dying too early are critically important life changing matters to people. Yet few people think about how they can protect themselves with disability insurance or life insurance until they're severely injured or terminally ill or one of their peers suddenly dies. If you straightforwardly ask a person where these priorities lie, they'll usually tell you they're extremely important. Why is it, then, that they're not important enough for them to naturally act upon?

We're often confused. We see death, disability, and infirmity as the travesties in and of life. Yet the fact is that every one of us will die. Many of us will become disabled and unable to work. Even more will live beyond our capacities to care for ourselves. These are the facts of life. They are life's realities. The travesty is that financial advisors leave their clients unprepared for them. And when people are left unprepared and the realities of life hit, their otherwise best laid plans go for naught. I don't blame the general public for failing to readily understand and appreciate this. Scary things like these are easier subjects to avoid than to face head-on. Advisors, on the other hand, can and should do a better job for their clients by asking the right questions that include what their clients want to have happen to those things they find of importance for their families and themselves when the realities of life come to pass. The answers to these questions will lead advisors to naturally call upon those financial tools that prepare their clients to face them.

Advisors who approach these topics appropriately do so without fear of rejection, as they find it unnecessary and even destructive to cling to a specific area of potential pain. This is when we serve our clients best—by helping them confront the things they may otherwise avoid, often to their detriment.

### TAKE THEM ON THAT JOURNEY

I like to say, "Tell me about your retirement and what's important about what you're doing and where you're doing it to make it enjoyable to you."

Take people into their future. Step them through the life ahead of them. Help them visualize it so they can paint the picture they want to live out. Author Cameron Herold (who *Forbes* magazine dubbed the "CEO Whisperer") reminds entrepreneurs to paint their vivid vision so that those around them, including staff, vendors, and other stakeholders, see it and help bring it to life. With entrepreneurs, that vision reflects the passionate resolve that drives them to build a company. As advisors, we're the architects of what our prospects and clients envision as their version of happiness, their lives fulfilled. The clearer we understand their vision of what that looks like, the easier it is for us to appreciate where they wish to go and how to best get them there. The easier it is, also, for us to articulate our understanding of what they want back to them. The better we as advisors do that, the deeper our prospects and clients can trust that what we're recommending is truly a step toward their hopes and intents. Helping them paint that picture makes it easier for them to accept the importance of adjusting what they're doing now and follow your recommendations for what they can do to make that possible.

People seldom do this for themselves. They seldom can. It's scary to think about what might happen in the future and to consider what you might do with the unknown facing you. With someone to help guide you forward and to confront the questions you must ask yourself, it's a whole lot easier and more productive. When you hold a prospect's hand and assure them that they can get through their fears and drive toward their hopes armed together with the proper plans of action to secure it all, they will find the courage to do what they need to do to really enjoy the things they want in their life.

People are often afraid to face their financial reality. They may have a vague image of their future life and believe they don't and won't have the finances to make what they want a reality. Rather than address the situation, they avoid it. As their advisor, you can do good by helping them find ways to confront this reality and create a fulfilled life that falls within their means.

When I look at what prospects want and then look at the facts of their current financial situations, getting everything they desire isn't always possible without some major changes. I lay these out in a way that helps them understand their options. Giving people this view empowers them to make better decisions. They can take a hard look at their priorities and think about how important these priorities really are and what they're willing to do or, sometimes, give up to get on a better track toward achieving what they truly seek to find happiness.

Maybe they'll get a new job that pays more, or maybe they'll save more of what they earn. Maybe they'll spend less on items of lesser priority to them. Sometimes they must adjust their vision of the future to match their reality. This doesn't have to be awful. It's a matter of looking at the priorities they identified and deciding which ones they're willing to cut back on, revise, or give up. They may defer the hopeful funding of that potential vacation home or change to what extent they help pay for their kids' graduate school expenses. They may choose to scale back the total amount of the inheritance they planned on leaving for the grandchildren. The important point of this is giving them that clear visibility into where they *really* are and their options for getting where they want to be. There's no hiding of the facts or wishful thinking. Without visualizing the future and how it will play out, they're simply putting off important decisions that are better off made sooner than later, so I do that hard work they've been putting off so they can make better choices that make their lives better.

When you take people on this journey, it's important to reserve all judgment. Lay out the facts of where they are relative to where they want to be and objectively show them alternative paths to get there. Provide them with the probability and potential of where the different options you recommend for their consideration may lead and how close they can expect to get to what they want to achieve by rearranging what they have. Your job is to get them to see their reality and offer your expert advice to help them get there efficiently and effectively. It's then up to them to make some very important and sometimes difficult decisions. When the considerations are aligned with what they find of most importance—what they're living for and would even die for—they'll make those decisions, and they'll be telling you, "Mahalo!", thankful to you for encouraging them to do so.

## BEING THE BEST ADVISOR FOR YOUR CLIENTS

This goes beyond educating them and hoping they'll do what's right. Think of your Ohana, your family members, and how you talk to them when they're faced with a tough decision that they're uncomfortable to confront. You're there to support them. If they continue to avoid the matter, do you help them avoid it, too? You don't, if you care about them and believe it's the right thing for them to do. You remind them of the reasons they find of importance that convinced them of their need to deal with that something and insist upon their doing whatever it is that's in their best interest to properly deal with it.

Not every advisor does this. It's not easy to do, and it's even more difficult to do it in a manner that's positioned for absolute success. When you truly care about your clients and you care about doing good, you'll want to do better for them. You'll want to do your best so they can live what they see as their best life.

That's what great financial advisors do. Beyond helping people discover what's important and offering your expert counsel, you keep them on track to do what they need to do to get what they want.

## THE HARD TRUTH

People are more willing to listen when they're faced with a hard truth that could have immediate ramifications. For example, I have a client who was diagnosed with terminal cancer. His top priority is providing for his wife. The man isn't very old, and his wife is several years younger, so he wants to ensure she has income for many years after his death.

Like many people, he did not expect to get cancer or have a plan for dying at such a young age, and he wishes he had started planning sooner. He and I talked, established what mattered most to him—his wife's quality of life after his passing—giving us a very clear target to shoot toward. Any financial decision this client makes can be measured against the effect it has on his ability to provide for his wife.

Remarkably, this man is thankfully in remission. In the meantime, the disease gave him laser focus on what was important to him, and it's put him in a better position financially moving forward. The fact that he's feeling healthy has his analytical mind constantly hoping to take advantage of markets and the like. It requires me to constantly remind him of what he continually states to be of highest importance to him—substantial guaranteed lifetime income to support the things of importance to his wife. He needs that reminder and always shares his gratitude for it. And, of course, he keeps this purposefully in mind as he tempers and guides his own investment-related decisions.

The story doesn't always go that way. I've had clients faced with hard truths who refused to act on them. I tend to blame myself when this happens. Could I have done something more to position myself better and choose my words more carefully to help them face their reality and do better with it? I suppose that when all is said and done, people need to take responsibility for their own choices. If it's not important enough to address to them, I shouldn't make it so important to me that I demand that they do so. That's imposing my opinion on others. That's a no-no.

## KŪLIA I KA NU'U

In your conversations with prospects and clients, don't shy away from the hard stuff. It's taming life's challenges to make life's hopes a reality that's truly rewarding anyway. Help people see the lives they desire, and don't be afraid to talk to them about their realities and the lives they currently enjoy. They're not always going to end up with that life they dream of living, but your expertise can help them figure out what's possible so you can begin the journey of realizing it together.

Stay on them. Remind them that issues as important as their family's security *must* be handled, and with great care. Let them know that even though life gets in the way, what matters to them is still important and worth their time and attention. They may not want to hear this at first. If they're willing to listen and face the truth, knowing that your intentions are pure, they'll be grateful to have you as their advisor and realize they have a true friend in you.

.

# ALOHA

Becoming an Aloha Advisor seems simple, and it is. It's not easy, though, especially at first. Advisors often tell me how hard it is to change the way they've been working with prospects and clients their whole careers. As they practice it, they soon realize that it's great for all kinds of situations in life, master it, and make it a part of their lives. You will, too.

Being an Aloha Advisor becomes easier as you practice it and experience the fruits—the sweetest grapes—of your labor. The hardest part is staying the course. You'll have moments of doubt where you might think it won't work. You may start to slide back to the traditional ways of financial advising—what you were taught and has worked for you to bring you the success you've found so far. That's normal. What I'm recommending seems too simple, too good to be true—I get it.

Trust. Stay the course and follow through. Practice, practice, practice, and you'll find advising people this way is the most natural thing in the world, because doing good is the more natural thing in the world. Your mind will flex as you adopt and adapt to it, and you'll become less judgmental and more grateful. You'll grow more curious and find people more interesting. Being an Aloha Advisor changes who you are and how you feel about your clients and everyone else, and others will sense this and feel differently about you, too.

People will appreciate you, and you'll feel good about yourself and what you're accomplishing. You'll see the difference you're making in people's lives, and it will change everything. Imagine making people happy. Imagine helping them enjoy better lives. Imagine getting paid well to do it.

By the way, getting paid well is the by-product of Aloha Advising for financial advisors. It's the bonus. Doing good to do well is the goal, and the lives you change for the better, and the life you better for yourself, are the payoff.

Not every advisor thinks this way. I've met some who think that if you teach aspiring advisors what they need to do to make a good income, they'll do those things. They believe that the key to success is knowing that income drives proper behavior. I don't agree. That may work; it's not the kind of life I want and not what I teach other advisors. For me, if I do the right things, I'm happy as I do them, and the money comes. I believe that the key to success is knowing that our behavior and what we do and how we do it drive income and my happiness. It's about doing right. It's about living my life with Mahalo, gratitude, and Aloha, love for everything and everyone. It's about Ohana, and treating people like family; Pono, and doing the right thing; and Imua—growing, learning, and moving forward. It's about becoming more compassionate and more valuable to the world and finding the courage to do more than I ever thought possible.

## A DAY IN THE LIFE OF AN ALOHA ADVISOR

You may be wondering what it's like to work like this, going through life with the principles of Mahalo, Aloha, Ohana, Pono, and Imua and being an Aloha Advisor. Let me tell you what it's like.

Imagine getting constant referrals to people who can't wait to see you and whom you're eager to meet. You know that each new prospect is ideal—a perfect match for what you do—and you receive each one of them with confidence, knowing you'll enjoy these people as clients and as friends.

You overhear your assistant confirming yet another appointment, even though your schedule is booked and she's going to struggle to find an opening. Your planner overflows with appointments with the new people you're going to meet. Your personal time is packed with the other people who are important to you—quality time you'll spend with family and friends.

Every day people smile at you in the hall, coming into your office and leaving, too. They send you those documents, complete that health assessment, and can't wait to meet with you again. This may seem like a charmed life. It's reality—my reality.

Every day, too, people thank me. They're grateful for what I do for them. I don't take their gratitude for granted, though. I learned many years ago that when a person becomes my client and thanks me, I'm in a position of influential power. I didn't figure this out myself—the concept comes from another author and speaker, Dr. Robert Cialdini.

I used to waste that moment. I'd say, "You're welcome," or

even respond with a simple, "Oh, it's nothing." I might say, "It was my pleasure," because in truth, it was. I eventually learned to use that moment as a stepping-stone to help more people. When people thank me, I ask them to introduce me to someone else whom I might enjoy working with as much as I enjoy them. I ask for a referral.

I don't ask them to introduce me to people who might need me for financial reasons, though that's how I was initially trained. For me, that's much too presumptuous. Instead, I ask them about people whom they know who are like them. My ideal clients then become my ideal advocates, and they introduce me to my ideal prospects. I'm an idealist, a dreamer. Because I'm not afraid to ask people for referrals at this perfect time of influential power, this dream of working with only ideal clients is indeed my reality.

I want clients who are caring, disciplined, and of high integrity and who believe in planning, committing to, and sticking to their plans of action. I want to meet new prospects whom my current ideal clients look up to and respect—people who are like them.

Let me tell you exactly how I do this. It's wonderful, and it works for me and for my clients, and for referred prospects, too.

It's not complicated. A new client thanks me for my efforts and I ask them to help me meet another person who's like them:

"You're welcome," I say, "and I want you to know how much I enjoy working with you and people like you. You know, people who care about themselves and those who depend on them.

Those who plan and then carry out those plans. People of integrity who do the things they say they're going to do, exactly the way they say they're going to do it. You know, people like you. Who do you know who's like that?"

Say I have a client, Joe, and we're putting the finishing touches on his initial wealth management strategy, and everything is working out exactly as planned. As he offers a handshake to thank me, I ask him for a referral, and he gives me the name of his good friend and colleague, Jane.

When I meet Jane, who is a prospect at that point, she's apprehensive. She doesn't openly trust advisors. Jane doesn't know me or my intentions, and I talk to her about how we came to meet: that I asked her friend, my client Joe, to tell me about a person he knows and respects. Who does he know that cares for their family and their business? Who cares about the people who depend on them? Who does he know of highest integrity who makes careful plans, puts those plans into action, and does what they say they'll do? You know, someone like him.

"Joe's immediate response was to give me your name, Jane," I tell her. "When I asked him for those he holds in highest esteem, you were the first person whom Joe thought of. So we both have Joe to thank for putting us together."

I meet amazing people this way, and I let them know up front how grateful I am to see them, and I tell them how they came to be referred to me. I tell them about the kind of people I like to work with—those of high integrity, and so on—and how, when I asked their friend if they knew anyone like that, they were the first person who came to mind.

After I meet with Jane, she'll likely call Joe and tell him how our visit went. Of course, our meeting focused solely on Jane and what's most important to her. Not only is she very happy about that meeting, but her friendship with Joe is stronger, because she now knows that Joe sees her in a very positive way. Joe feels this, too, and when I ask him for more referrals, he's happy to provide them. He may even call to recommend people to me.

Getting referrals in this way works exceedingly well. In fact, when I started doing it, I ended up with more referrals, and more leads, than I could handle. When I left Hawaii to open new offices, I left a box full of a mixed bag of general leads to other advisors, who were kind enough to manage them for me. When you're getting started, it's vital to have more leads than you know you can handle. You do anything to be more comfortable and confident as you fight to successfully face another day. Today, I wouldn't be able to do that, as my clients now come by way of referrals. I prize referrals, and I only take what I have time for among those people with the behavioral attitudes I just shared, because every person deserves their advisor's undivided and immediate attention.

This is how I grow my business with people I care about and enjoy—people who invigorate and inspire me and make every day an opportunity to share Aloha.

## ALOHA MEANS GOODBYE

Each of us comes into the world with a family and a history. I'm grateful for my family and the foundation they provided for me to make my way in this world. For many years, I wasn't fully aware of my family's history or that of my people, Americans of Japanese ancestry.

My paternal grandfather, L. T. Kagawa, challenged racially discriminatory practices and introduced life insurance policies for people of color in 1930s Hawaii. His hard work and success amid the Great Depression made it possible for my father to live a good life and enjoy a good education.

My father, Siegfred "Sig" Kagawa, a third-generation American of Japanese ancestry, welcomed me into his master agency and gave me the opportunity to learn the business of wealth management. He and my mother, Betsy Yamashita Kagawa, ingrained in me the values by which I continue to do my best to live my life: Mahalo, Aloha, Ohana, Pono, and Imua.

My parents, Siegfred "Sig" and Betsy Kagawa, 1994, in Montreux, Switzerland, where my father and the Kagawa family were named "Legends of Transamerica."

It took time and much more experience to understand and appreciate the blessings of being shaped by this growing up. I never understood or valued this earlier in my life and instead fought valiantly against it. It wasn't until much later that I learned about my maternal grandfather, Hirokichi Yamashita, and my paternal great-grandfather, Yonekichi Kagawa, who both came from Hiroshima. My paternal great-grandfather actually returned to Hiroshima during that fateful time during WWII and survived the bombings.

Yonekichi, a first-generation American of Japanese ancestry, arrived in the United States from Hiroshima in 1894 as part of an agreement between the Kingdom of Hawaii and Japanese Imperial Government to provide laborers to Hawaii. He worked in the plantations, perhaps digging irrigation ditches that carried water to the sugarcane fields or working directly in them. Eventually he ran away from the camps on the Big Island, stowed away on a boat, and ended up in Lahaina, Maui. There, he became a bartender; met my great-grandmother, Kiyo Higashi; and saved enough money to buy a house. He converted the place into a very modest hotel in 1903—the first hotel in Kahului, Maui. He eventually went back to Hiroshima, and faced the bombing that ended WWII, before returning to the States. In the meantime, their son, my grandfather L. T., opened his business in 1933.

During World War II, L. T. and his family—including my father, his mother, and four of his five sisters (sister Carol was not yet born)—were among the nearly 120,000 Americans of Japanese ancestry who were taken from their homes and isolated behind barbed wire in internment camps at the fateful unveiling of Executive Order 9066. At the time, there were about the same number in Hawaii, and it wasn't practical for the government to imprison all of them, though they did send about 800 to what are now identified as concentration camps (not to be confused with death camps) in some of the most desolate wastelands across the United States. The Kagawas were included in this select group. Their final destination was Jerome, Arkansas.

The concentration camp in Jerome, Arkansas, where my family was held during World War II.

My family standing just outside the concentration camp in Jerome, Arkansas. The photo was taken in 1942, and though the photographer may have found a pleasant backdrop, the guard tower is clearly visible in the distance. Back row from left to right: Auntie Betty (Fujioka), Grandpa L. T. Kagawa, Grandma Ayako Kagawa, Auntie June (Reinwald). Front row from left to right: Auntie Joy (Tanaka), Dad Sig Kagawa, Auntie May (Murata).

I learned about this after my father became involved with the Japanese American National Museum. I couldn't understand why he was dedicating so much time to this cause. I didn't know what was taken from my family and what they had endured, or what the words "Go for Broke" meant. Today I'm committed to sharing this too-little-known and extremely important American story. I do it to honor those who made the trek to our country in search of the promises of American democracy, who became rightful Americans and then endured its broken promises. I do it to share how a community regained its rights as citizens to ultimately succeed by rising above the hypocrisy of poor decisions fueled by fear and hysteria and by choosing to live with honor, humility, loyalty, and belief in the very country that chose to turn its back on it. Sure, it's much more personal to me since it involved my family and those from my ancestral home. More important to me is that we remember our mistakes to avoid repeating them. It's the right thing to do.

When the Japanese bombed Pearl Harbor, those of Japanese blood in America were looked upon and officially categorized as "enemy" and "non-aliens," even though they were citizens of the United States. Yet they created a volunteer group that eventually led to the formation of the 100th Battalion and the 442nd Regimental Combat Unit and, along with those of Japanese blood and tongue serving in the Military Intelligence Service, fought for America in spite of the poor decisions imposed upon them by the US government. They were sent to the worst places during the war, yet they kept winning their battles for the very government that incarcerated them, and theirs is still recognized as the most highly decorated unit for its size and duration in US military history.

My parents never explained this to me. Looking back at what

my father's family survived and what they accomplished shows me that despite my family's humble and often difficult beginnings in America, they believed and trusted, stood loyally by its promises, and thrived.

The opportunities I enjoyed—and that I still enjoy—were due in large part to the entrepreneurship, relentless drive, and endurance of my forefathers. As a boy growing up in Hawaii, I enjoyed my freedom and racial equality and even shared a high school classroom with a person who would eventually become president of the United States, Barack Obama.

Earlier in my life, I took all of this for granted. Instead of doing everything within my power to live up to the high standards set by my family, I failed in many ways. I squandered my opportunities and even dropped out of college, a decision that for many years became the bane of my existence. I let my immediate family and those from prior generations who sacrificed for me down. I developed a chip on my shoulder and fought hard to make up for that mistake. The choices we make define us. I can never make up for those of the past.

Despite my mistakes, I met people along the way who believed in me. Blessed with the core values that my parents had instilled in me, I leaned on their valuable guidance to rise above my past and focus on making the right decision in each new moment. This is my hope for you as well—to realize that no matter what you've done in the past, your legacy can change now. Today. This moment.

I continue my journey toward becoming the person—the son, the grandson, and the great-grandson—I aspire to be, one worthy of my family legacy. You're welcome to join me on this journey, too, a journey of doing good to do better for yourself, for your clients, and for anyone else whose life you touch. Over the years, I've created my own companies, which are dedicated to helping people and companies financially navigate internationally between Asia and the United States. My goal is to take international wealth management and financial planning—which currently operates in siloes, nation by nation—to the next level. Thanks to the transparency of new laws, I believe my vision of global financial navigation is possible. It's my future and yours, with no walls between nations to inhibit optimum wealth opportunity and management.

My mission here in the US is to shape the way financial planning is delivered to our multinational realities. I do so by focusing on helping first-generation, ethnic Asian families acclimate to their new American homes by connecting them with advisors across banking, insurance, investments, tax, and law from around the Pacific. I wish to deliver financial planning that flexes to the reality of the US, a land of immigrants from about 200 nations, and to honor and address the realities of where we come from and to where we roam. My companies are anxious to help shape and deliver best practices within the world of international wealth management.

I don't expect to match the legacies of my great-grandfather, my grandfather, my father, or my mother. Now, when I hear the phrase "standing on the shoulders of giants," I get it. To me, these people were giants. Their struggles were much greater than mine. I only hope that, in time and through people of shared belief, we might work together to architect a new world of global finance and wealth management that brings access and opportunities to even more people. To *everyone*. I'd like to believe that by working this way with others, I might make my own small, meaningful contribution to the Kagawa name and legacy.

At the end of the day—at the end of our *lives*—the footprints we leave behind reflect the choices we've made. They show the rest of the world who we were, what we believed in, and what we stood for. If we choose to be advisors and make it our life's work, the work done and how we did it becomes our legacy—the footprints we leave behind.

Becoming an Aloha Financial Advisor is worth doing. It's about the pursuit of happiness, and how you achieve it by helping others achieve their happiness. It's about creating a life that's worth living, one that will make you glad you chose this profession. It's one of many ways to act as an advisor, and while it may or may not be your way, it's what I believe in. Throughout the years and around the world, it has served me well. I believe it can serve you well, too.

Thank you for reading my book. If you agree with my philosophy, I hope you'll adopt it and share it with other people—other financial advisors, your prospective clients, and those who count on us, on *you*, to help them enjoy more fulfilled lives. Tell them, "This is how I do what I do. If you find my way of doing things agreeable, I'd be delighted to have the opportunity to be of potential value and help to you. If you find my way of doing things agreeable, perhaps we could work together someday." If you do this, let me know. Tell me what you're doing to progress this new way of financial advising and how you're building this new world of Aloha Advising around the globe. Maybe you and I will someday work together, too.

Ultimately, what makes you an Aloha Advisor will come from

you. Who are you as a person? What values drive you? Do you want to make the world a better place? Do you want to change other people's lives for the better? Think about the kind of person you want to be. No matter what decisions you've made in the past and what your footprints say about you, you can change your path today. The footprints you leave behind can lead wherever you decide to go. You can be happy and lead a truly fulfilled life, knowing that you're creating a legacy you believe in. One that respects your potential and doesn't take who you are—and who you can *become*—for granted.

Think it over. Figure out what it is that will bring the Aloha out of you. Write it down. Define it and make it your mission. Allow it to direct your work. Commit to sharing it, spreading it, putting it out there—getting the real you into everything you do. Doing that is more powerful than anything I can teach you.

# ACKNOWLEDGMENTS

At the end of the day, it's the values by which we choose to live our lives that make all the difference.

Thank you to my mother, Betsy, and father, Sig. Though I fought it for a good part of my life, the values you've instilled in me continue to emerge from that which you ingrained inside of me. As my understanding and appreciation of these values deepen, it's illuminating a brighter pathway of choices for me and my life. Mom and Dad, you allowed me to share that Aloha with others. May it lead them toward better places, too.

So many people have made an impact on my life, too numerous to mention. Thank you to anyone whose path has crossed my own. Whether it was a pleasant or an unpleasant part of our journeys, in some way, you shaped the person I've become, and I am forever grateful.

I'm truly blessed.

# ABOUT THE AUTHOR

**STEPHEN KAGAWA** is CEO of The Pacific Bridge Companies, where he helps financial advisors and their clients in navigating the global financial environment. Working with the collaborative OhanaNet, he connects advisors across the disciplines of banking, insurance, investments, tax, and the law.

Stephen is also a trustee on the board of the Japanese American National Museum, an organization based on the experiences of Japanese Americans from immigration through World War II and which celebrates multi-ethnic diversity and its outcomes today. He's also the past chair of the Go For Broke National Education Center, which honors the Japanese American Nisei soldiers of World War II who rose up to become the most decorated units in US military history. Stephen was a founding member of the board of the US-Japan Council, which seeks to strengthen US-Japan relations by connecting leaders from both countries. He is also a Baden-Powell Fellow for the World Scouting Foundation and an active member of the Million Dollar Round Table Foundation, an association for financial professionals that promotes and supports other organizations and nonprofits that bring value to its members worldwide.

When he's not sharing Aloha with his clients, enjoying his staff and their dogs at his dog-friendly office, volunteering for a nonprofit organization, or contributing to one of his many favorite charities, Stephen enjoys good food, good friends, red wine, and live music. He dabbles in songwriting—mostly love ballads—and is a fan of all teams Hawaiian and University of Southern California.

Although he's partial to the West Coast and the islands of Hawaii, Stephen's greatest passion is traveling the world and exploring local culture. In his free time, you're more likely to find him at a market or a side-street café than in a high-end restaurant, discovering what people in other areas of the world eat, drink, and do in their own pursuits of happiness.

Stephen lives in Southern California.